Early Views on Music and Ethics

Books by David Whitwell

The Sousa Oral History Project
The Art of Musical Conducting
The Longy Club: 1900–1917
La Téléphonie and the Universal Musical Language
Extraordinary Women
A Concise History of the Wind Band
Essays on the Modern Wind Band
Essays on Performance Practice
A New History of Wind Music
The College and University Band
The Early Symphonies of Mozart
Music of the French Revolution
Stories from the Podium

On Composers
Wagner on Bands
Berlioz on Bands
Chopin: A Self-Portrait
Liszt: A Self-Portrait
Schumann: A Self-Portrait in His Own Words
Mendelssohn: A Self-Portrait in His Own Words

On Education
Philosophic Foundations of Education
Foundations of Music Education
Music Education of the Future

Aesthetics of Music

Aesthetics of Music in Ancient Civilizations
Aesthetics of Music in the Middle Ages
Aesthetics of Music in the Early Renaissance
Aesthetics of Music in Sixteenth-Century Italy, France and Spain
Aesthetics of Music in Sixteenth-Century Germany, the Low Countries and England
Aesthetics of Baroque Music in Italy, Spain, the German-Speaking Countries and the Low Countries
Aesthetics of Baroque Music in France
Aesthetics of Baroque Music in England

The History and Literature of the Wind Band and Wind Ensemble Series

Volume 1 The Wind Band and Wind Ensemble Before 1500
Volume 2 The Renaissance Wind Band and Wind Ensemble
Volume 3 The Baroque Wind Band and Wind Ensemble
Volume 4 The Wind Band and Wind Ensemble of the Classical Period (1750–1800)
Volume 5 The Nineteenth-Century Wind Band and Wind Ensemble
Volume 6 A Catalog of Multi-Part Repertoire for Wind Instruments or for Undesignated Instrumentation before 1600
Volume 7 Baroque Wind Band and Wind Ensemble Repertoire
Volume 8 Classical Period Wind Band and Wind Ensemble Repertoire
Volume 9 Nineteenth-Century Wind Band and Wind Ensemble Repertoire
Volume 10 A Supplementary Catalog of Wind Band and Wind Ensemble Repertoire
Volume 11 A Catalog of Wind Repertoire before the Twentieth Century for One to Five Players
Volume 12 A Second Supplementary Catalog of Early Wind Band and Wind Ensemble Repertoire
Volume 13 Name Index, Volumes 1–12, The History and Literature of the Wind Band and Wind Ensemble

Ancient Voices

Ancient Views on Music and Religion
Ancient Views on the Natural World
Ancient Views on What Is Music
Contemporary Descriptions of Early Musicians
Early Views of Music and Ethics
Early Thoughts on Performance Practice
Music Performance in Ancient Societies

Renaissance Voices

Essays on Renaissance Philosophies of Music
Renaissance Men on Music

www.whitwellbooks.com

David Whitwell

Ancient Voices
Views on Music by Ancient and
Medieval Writers

Early Views on Music and Ethics

Edited by Craig Dabelstein

WHITWELL PUBLISHING • AUSTIN, TEXAS, USA

Ancient Voices: Views on music by ancient and medieval writers
Early Views on Music and Ethics
Dr. David Whitwell

WHITWELL PUBLISHING
AUSTIN, TX 78701
WWW.WHITWELLPUBLISHING.COM

© 2013 by David Whitwell
All rights reserved. First edition 2013

Composed in Bembo Book.
Published in the United States of America.
All images used in this book are in the public domain except where otherwise noted.

ISBN-13: 9781936512775

Cover design by Daniel Ferla.

Contents

	Acknowledgement	ix
Part 1:	On the Philosophy of Music and Ethics	
1	On Music and Character Formation	3
2	On Music and Manners	23
3	On the Character of the Performer	39
4	Women not Allowed	47
Part 2:	On Ethics and Performance	
5	Ancient Artists and the Public	65
6	Renaissance Artists and the Public	81
7	Baroque Artists and the Public	93
8	Nineteenth-Century Artists and the Public	103
9	Early Views on Criticism	117
	Bibliography	133
	About the Author	143
	About the Editor	145

Acknowledgments

I am indebted to my friend and colleague, Craig Dabelstein, for his help in preparing this book for publication.

David Whitwell
Austin, Texas

PART I
ON THE PHILOSOPHY OF MUSIC AND ETHICS

On Music and Character Formation

> It is quite regrettable that none of us now knows
> what constitutes *Musica moralis*.
>
> Johann Mattheson (1681–1764)

THE GREEK WORD, 'ETHOS,' HAD TO DO WITH CHARACTER. In a play or oration it meant establishing the character of the individual as it is seen by the observer, as opposed to the actor's actions. The original Greek meaning was 'the place of living,' or what we might think of as 'the person inside.' From this one can understand that in the context of ancient Greek education this word meant the education of the *character* of the student. In English the definition sometimes given for 'ethos' is 'theory of living,' a typical modern practical definition. It is from this meaning that the English word 'ethics' derives.

The almost exclusive use of music for the purpose of forming the character of the student was an educational principle believed and acted on for thousands of years. And yet, what music teacher in our time will dare speak of this subject in class? How many music teachers today make this priority number one in the selection of repertoire for their students to study and perform?

The present essay looks at the ancient discussion of this topic. The following essay deals with music and manners, which we take to mean the student's actions *after* his character formation has taken place.

Of the ancient Egyptian people who pre-date the ancient Greeks, our primary record is the tomb paintings. Very little literature exists, but references by the later Greeks give us a few clues regarding the use of music in that earlier society. It is an important question for it appears that much of the character of the ancient Greek society, including music, came from Egypt. Strabo, for example, writing during the first years of the Christian Era, says that the Egyptians instructed their children with music established by the government and that musicians were in charge of the development of character in the young.[1]

> The musicians in giving instruction in singing and playing the lyre or aulos considered this virtue as essential, since they maintain that such studies are destined to create discipline and develop the character.[2]

---

[1] This remains true today, however, today neither the teachers nor the parents have any idea who the musicians are who are forming the character of their children.

[2] Quoted in Lise Manniche, *Music and Musicians in Ancient Egypt* (London: British Museum Press, 1991), 41. Plato's span of 10,000 years is not possible as that would extend back to the time of the primitive cave paintings.

Once the Egyptians arrived at their educational principles, including those relative to character formation, sources tell us the government prohibited any further changes or additions. Plato (427–347 BC) mentions that this was true for all the arts, including music. Speaking of Egypt, in his *Laws* he reports,

> Long ago they appear to have recognized the very principle of which we are now speaking—that their young citizens must be habituated to forms and strains of virtue. These they fixed, and exhibited the patterns of them in their temples; and no painter, no other representative artist is allowed to innovate upon them, or to leave the traditional forms and invent new ones. To this day, no alteration is allowed either in these arts, or in music at all. And you find that their works of art are painted or molded in the same forms which they had ten thousand years ago;—this is literally true and no exaggeration,—their ancient paintings and sculptures are not a bit better or worse than the works of today, but are made with just the same skill.[3]

We can assume Plato to be a good source here as he personally studied in Egypt for nineteen years.

His discussion of the history of music practice in Greece implies that he had some knowledge of its earlier history as well as we can see in his first sentence:

> Let us speak of the laws about music,—that is to say, such music as then existed,—in order that we may trace the growth of the excess of freedom from the beginning.[4]

He begins with a brief history of some of the musical forms associated with the cult-religious practices and then becomes considerably more animated when he speaks of the audience.

> All these forms and others were duly distinguished, nor were the performers allowed to confuse one style of music with another. And the authority which determined and gave judgment, and punished the disobedient, was not expressed in a hiss, nor in the most unmusical shouts of the multitude, as in our days, nor in applause and clapping of hands. But the directors of public instruction insisted that the spectators should listen in silence to the end; and boys and their tutors, and the multitude in general, were kept quiet by a hint from a stick. Such was the good order which the multitude were willing to observe; they would never have dared to give judgment by noisy cries.

From this it is already apparent that Plato believed that the greatest period of Greek music, culturally speaking, was already past. He blames the musicians, composers and performers themselves, for this decay and squarely places the blame on them for seeking to please the audience without any perceptions of the subsequent danger to their art.

> And then, as time went on, the [singing] poets themselves introduced the reign of vulgar and lawless innovation. They were men of genius, but they had no perception of what is just and lawful in music; raging like bacchanals and possessed with inordinate delights—mingling lamentations with hymns, and paeans with dithyrambs; imitating the sounds of the flute on the lyre, and making one

---

3 *Laws*, trans. B. Jowett (Oxford: Clarendon Press, 1953), 656d. Most, if not all, of the writings of Plato are assumed to be information he was passing down from an earlier generation, from Socrates.

4 *Laws*, 656d.

general confusion; ignorantly affirming that music has no truth, and, whether good or bad, can only be judged of rightly by the pleasure of the hearer. And by composing such licentious works, and adding to them words as licentious, they have inspired the multitude with lawlessness and boldness, and made them fancy that they can judge for themselves about melody and song. And in this way the theaters from being silent have become vocal, as though they had understanding of good and bad in music and poetry; and instead of an aristocracy, an evil sort of theatrocracy has grown up. For if there had been a democracy in music alone, consisting of free men, no fatal harm would have been done; but in music there first arose the universal conceit of omniscience and general lawlessness;—freedom came following afterwards, and men, fancying that they knew what they did not know, had no longer any fear, and the absence of fear begets shamelessness. For what is this shamelessness, which is so evil a thing, but the insolent refusal to regard the opinion of the better by reason of an over-daring sort of liberty?[5]

The ancient Greeks also placed great emphasis on the use of music to form the character of the young. In a widely quoted definition, Plato wrote,

> Education has two branches,—one of gymnastic, which is concerned with the body, and the other of music, which is designed for the improvement of the soul.[6]

For Plato it was in this area of the improvement of the soul where he found the great value of music education. The importance of the educational value of this mysterious art of music, which could not even be seen, was first based on an idea shared by other early philosophers, that while the other senses, smell, touch, taste and sight all seemed to be a form of information outside the body and therefore accessible to discussion, music seemed to enter through the ears to affect us inside the body reaching the heart, meaning our feelings. Second, since the feelings heard in the music were by nature so similar to those felt in the heart, it followed that an educational pedagogy based on imitation, or modeling, held the promise of improving the character of the listener. This was why Plato sensed the great power of music.

> Therefore musical training is a more potent instrument than any other, because rhythm and harmony find their way into the inward places of the soul, on which they mightily fasten, imparting grace, and making the soul of him who is rightly educated graceful, or of him who is ill-educated ungraceful; and also because he who has received this true education of the inner being will most shrewdly perceive omissions or faults in art and nature, and with a true taste, while he praises and rejoices over and receives into his soul the good, and becomes noble and good, he will justly blame and hate the bad, now in the days of his youth, even before he is able to know the reason why; and when reason comes he will recognize and salute the friend with whom his education has made him long familiar.
> Yes, he said, I quite agree with you in thinking that it is for such reasons that they should be trained in music.[7]

---

5 Ibid., 700ff.

6 Ibid, 795d.

7 *Republic*, 401d. Because of the power of this modeling, Plato also added that probably too much music, as well as too much gymnastics, was probably undesirable. Aristotle agrees with this basic pedagogy in *Problemata*, 920b.28.

It followed, demonstrating the significance Plato gave music education, that he recognized the value of the teachers, urging the state to find the best teachers, even importing them from other lands and providing them with houses and good pay. Children, Plato contends, should attend whether or not the parents approved.

Regarding the kind of music to be used in education, we unfortunately are without much detail due to the fact that Plato had very little technical knowledge of music, a fact he readily admitted.[8] He did believe it should be simple, rather than complex[9]; should have virtue[10] and above all have verisimilitude.[11] This last quality, that music must be True, was illustrated by Plato in analogies meaningful to his audience. For our time Truth might better represent music which is genuine, as opposed to the constructed music of the educational publishers. 'No trickery,' says Plato![12]

On the other hand, Plato was very clear about the kinds of music which were not appropriate for use in music education. Popularity is not a critera[13] and not just whatever kind of music the students want.[14] Indeed he speaks at length on the bad educational influence which comes from popular music.[15] Four hundred years later one of the last of the ancient Greek philosophers, Philodemus, first century AD, still reflected this basic contention. Music, he wrote, which is devoid of significance naturally 'equates with disorderliness and lack of restraint.'[16]

It would appear that the old basic educational values regarding the use of music continued for some time. Plutarch (46–119 AD) recalled that the Greeks 'were so careful to teach their children music,'

> for they deemed it requisite by the assistance of music to form and compose the minds of youth to what was decent, sober, and virtuous; believing the use of music beneficially efficacious to incite to all serious actions.[17]

Strabo, writing at about the same time, mentioned the divine connection.

> They assumed that every form of music is the work of the gods ... And by the same course of reasoning they also attribute to music the upbuilding of morals, believing that everything which tends to correct the mind is close to the gods.[18]

---

8   Ibid., 400. Here he recommends another teacher, Damon, who could answer such questions.

9   *Laws*, 812b.

10 *Republic*, III, 397c.

11 *Laws*, 668c.

12 Ibid.

13 *Republic*, III, 397c.

14 *Laws*, 656f and 659d.

15 Ibid.

16 Warren D. Anderson, *Ethos and Education in Greek Music* (Cambridge: Harvard University Press, 1966), 153.

17 'Concerning Music.'

18 Strabo, *The Geography of Strabo*, trans. Horace L. Jones (Cambridge: Harvard University Press, 1960), X.3.10.

Athenaeus, a source of very extensive information in the older Greek civilization, as evidenced in the following by his reference to Damon of Athens, the teacher of Socrates, dwells on the fact that the ancient Greeks were very selective regarding the quality of the music used for forming the character of the young.

> Music contributes also to the exercise and the sharpening of the mind; hence all Greeks as well as those barbarians [those who do not speak Greek well!] with whom we are acquainted make use of it. With good reason Damon of Athens and his school say that songs and dances are the result of the soul's being in a kind of motion; those songs which are noble and beautiful produce noble and beautiful souls, whereas the contrary kind produce the contrary. Whence also came that witty remark of Cleosthenes, the ruler of Sicyon, which reveals his cultivated mind. For, as they say, after seeing one of his daughter's suitors dancing in vulgar posture he declared that he had 'danced away' his marriage, probably believing that the young man's soul was also vulgar. For, whether in dancing or in walking, decency and dignity of bearing are beautiful, whereas immodesty and vulgarity are ugly. For this reason, in fact, from the very beginning, the poets arranged dances for freemen, and they used the dance figures only to illustrate the theme of the songs, always preserving nobility and manliness in them.... But if any one arranged his figures with undue exaggeration, or when he came to his songs said anything that did not correspond to the dance, he was discredited.[19]

Strabo also confirmed this, saying of them, 'that music was ever accounted among them the best, which was most grave, simple and natural.'[20]

One of the characteristics of the ancient Greek philosophy of music education was their belief that if the child's character was formed early through the appropriate music, his character became 'set' for life. Plato once wrote regarding how this affected the child's music preferences later on.

> And if a man be brought up from childhood to the age of discretion and maturity in the use of the orderly and severe music, when he hears the opposite he detests it, and calls it illiberal; but if trained in the sweet and vulgar music, he deems the severer kind cold and displeasing. So that while he who hears them gains no more pleasure from the one than from the other, the one has the advantage of making those who are trained in it better men, whereas the other makes them worse.[21]

This subject is also mentioned by Plutarch. He writes that Aristoxenus (b. ca. 350 BC), a pupil of both the Pythagorean School and of Aristotle, spoke about the value of music in forming character in some books which are now lost, but were known to Plutarch. Plutarch passes on to us, from these lost books of Aristoxenus, a discussion regarding the lyric poets, who were before Socrates. Then he tells about Telesias the Theban to demonstrate that proper lessons once learned become part of the character and cannot be easily changed.

---

[19] Athenaeus, *Deipnosophistae*, XIV, 628.
[20] 'Concerning Music.'
[21] *Laws*, 802.

> Now that the right molding or ruin of ingenuous manners and civil conduct lies in a well-grounded musical education, Aristoxenus has made apparent. For, of those that were contemporary with him, he gives an account of Telesias the Theban, who in his youth was bred up in the noblest excellences of music, and moreover studied the works of the most famous lyric poets, Pindar, Dionysius the Theban, Lamprus, Pratinas, and all the rest who were accounted most eminent; who played also to perfection upon the aulos, and was not a little industrious to furnish himself with all those other accomplishments of learning; but being past the prime of his age, he was so bewitched with the theater's new fangles and the innovations of multiplied notes, that despising those noble precepts and that solid practice to which he had been educated, he betook himself to Philoxenus and Timotheus, and among those delighted chiefly in such as were most depraved with diversity of notes and baneful innovation. And yet, when he made it his business to make verses and labor both ways, as well in that of Pindar as that of Philoxenus, he could have no success in the latter. And the reason proceeded from the truth and exactness of his first education.[22]

In the only surviving fragments of Aristoxenus' writing which mentions this point, he is a bit more guarded with respect to music and education.

> Some consider music [*harmonie*] a sublime science, and expect a course of it to make them musicians; nay some even conceive it will exalt their moral nature. This mistake is due to their having run away with such phrases in our preamble as ... 'one class of musical art is hurtful to the moral character, another improves it'; while they missed completely our qualification of this statement, 'in so far as musical art can improve the moral character.'[23]

Aristotle (384–322 BC), the great philosopher who followed Plato, not only believed in the use of music to form the character of the young, but he believed that of the five senses hearing (music) is the *only* one which can affect character.

> Why is it that of all things which are perceived by the senses that which is heard alone possesses moral character? For music, even if it is unaccompanied by words, yet has character; whereas a color and an odor and taste have not.[24]

This seems to have been an ancient idea. The fifth century BC historian, Herodotus, quotes Xerxes, the fifth century BC King of Persia as declaring,

> Mark my words: it is through the ears you can touch a man to pleasure or rage—let the spirit which dwells there hear good things, and it will fill the body with delight; let it hear bad, and it will swell with fury.[25]

For Aristotle the means by which music education affects character lies, as in the case of the experience of Tragedy, in catharsis. When we hear emotions in music our feelings move in sympathy.

---

[22] Quoted by Plutarch in 'Concerning Music.'

[23] Aristoxenus, *The Elements of Harmony*, 16, trans., Henry S. Macran (Hildesheim: Georg Olms Verlag, 1974), 31.

[24] 'Problemata,' 919b.26.

[25] Herodotus, *The Histories*, VII, 37.

> Rhythm and melody supply imitations of anger and gentleness, and also of courage and temperance, and of all the qualities contrary to these, and of the other qualities of character, which hardly fall short of the actual emotions, as we know from our own experience, for in listening to such strains our souls undergo a change. The habit of feeling pleasure or pain at mere representations is not far removed from [the real feelings].[26]

The key in making this work, according to Aristotle, was in the selection of the highest music. Only certain kinds of music produce the catharsis with the empathy and introspection (pity and fear) necessary to character formation.

> We accept the division of melodies ... into ethical melodies, melodies of action, and passionate or inspiring melodies, each having, as they say, a mode corresponding to it ...
>
> In education the most ethical modes are to be preferred, but in listening to the performances of others we may admit the modes of action and passions also. For feelings such as pity and fear, or, again, enthusiasm, exist very strongly in some souls, and have more or less influence over all. Some persons fall into a religious frenzy, whom we see as a result of the sacred melodies—when they have used the melodies that excite the soul to mystic frenzy—restored as through they had found healing and purgation. Those who are influenced by pity and fear, and every emotional nature, must have a like experience, and others in so far as each is susceptible to such emotions, and all are in a manner purged and their souls lightened and delighted. The purgative melodies likewise give an innocent pleasure to mankind.[27]

Specifically it is the style of the Dorian people that he finds most effective.[28]

> But for education the ethical modes should be used, such as Dorian ... All men agree that the Dorian music is the gravest and manliest. And whereas we say that the extremes should be avoided and the mean followed, and whereas the Dorian is a mean between the other modes, it is evident that our youth should be taught the Dorian music.[29]

In another place he mentions the Dorian and other peoples' music with regard to their character.

> Even in mere melodies there is an imitation of character, for the musical modes differ essentially from one another, and those who hear them are differently affected by each. Some of them make men sad and grave, like the so-called Mixolydian, others enfeeble the mind, like the relaxed modes, another, again, produces a moderate and settled temper, which appears to be the peculiar effect of the Dorian; the Phrygian inspires enthusiasm. The whole subject has been well treated by philosophical writers on this branch of education, and they confirm their arguments by facts.[30]

---

[26] *Politica*, 1340a.19.

[27] *Politica*, 1342a . The music of some of these peoples was apparently so associated with particular forms that Aristotle cites [1342b.] an instance of a performer who attempted to perform a dithyramb, 'acknowledged to be Phrygian,' in the Dorian and could not do it.

[28] The reader is reminded that these are not references to the later 'church modes,' one of which is also called Dorian. Here they refer to actual peoples and their music.

[29] *Politica*, 1342a.27 and 1342b.14.

[30] Ibid., 1340a.40. The 'facts' Aristotle refers to here are unknown to us.

This same effect happens in viewing paintings, he says, but to a lesser extent. 'Even still the young should be taught to look at [only] the best art.'

As for music of lesser quality, it still has a place.

> Such are the modes and the melodies in which those who perform music at the theater should be invited to compete. But since the spectators are of two kinds—the one free and educated, and the other a vulgar crowd composed of mechanics, laborers, and the like—there ought to be contests and exhibitions instituted for the relaxation of the second class also ... A man receives pleasure from what is natural to him, and therefore professional musicians may be allowed to practice this lower sort of music before an audience of a lower type.[31]

No early writer addresses this topic with more heartfelt passion than the great historian Polybius (200–188 BC). He departs from his description of the internal wars of the period 220–216 BC to give a fervent testimonial to the very practical role music plays in shaping the character of entire peoples. It is an important testimonial to the educational use of music by the ancient Greeks. The reader will notice here again the emphasis on *quality* music. 'I mean *true* music,' as Polybius calls it.

Why, Polybius asks, did the savage character of the Cynaethans so far surpass all the other Greeks of that period in cruelty and lawless behavior?

> My own opinion is that they were the first and indeed the only people among the Arcadians to have abandoned an institution which had been nobly conceived by their ancestors, and was studied by all the inhabitants of Arcadia in their relation to their natural conditions. I am referring here to the special attention given to music, and by this I mean true music, which is a blessing to all peoples, but in the case of the Arcadians, a necessity. We should certainly not accept the suggestion of Ephorus, who threw into the preface to his history a sentence that was quite unworthy of him, to the effect that music was introduced among men merely for the purpose of beguiling and deceiving one another. Nor should we imagine that the Cretans and the Lacedaemonians did not have good reason for substituting the use of the aulos and of rhythmic movements in place of the trumpets in their military operations. In the same way the early Arcadians knew what they were about when they gave music such an important place in their public life that not only boys but young men up to the age of thirty were obliged to study it constantly, even though in other respects they lived under the most austere conditions. For it is a fact that is well-attested and familiar to all that Arcadia is almost the only nation in which the boys are taught from their earliest childhood to sing in measure the hymns and paeans in which they commemorate, according to their traditions, the gods and heroes of particular localities.
>
> Later they learn the measures of Philoxenus and Timotheus, and every year in the theater there are keenly contested competitions in choral singing to the accompaniment of professional aulos players, the boys taking part in the events which are suitable to their age and then men in what is called the men's festival.
>
> And in addition to these occasions, it is their custom all through their lives to entertain themselves at their banquets: they do not listen to hired performers but create their own music, each man being called upon for a song in turn. They are not at all ashamed to admit that they are completely ignorant of other studies, but in the case of singing nobody can claim to be untaught because everybody is obliged to learn; nor can they say that they know not how to sing, or excuse themselves from per-

---

[31] Ibid., 1342a.17.

forming, for this would be considered a disgrace among them. Besides this, the young men practice marching melodies on the aulos while they are on parade, perfect themselves in dances, and give annual displays in the theaters, all these activities being carried on through the patronage of the state and at the public expense.

In introducing these practices I do not believe that the ancestors of the Arcadians thought of them as luxuries or extravagances. On the contrary, they saw that personal manual labor was the general lot, that the life of the people was toilsome and hard, and that as a natural consequence of the country's cold and gloomy climate the character of its inhabitants was correspondingly austere. The fact is that as mortal men we adapt ourselves by sheer necessity to climatic influences, and it is this reason and no other which causes separate nations and peoples dwelling widely apart to differ so markedly in their circumstances, their physique and their complexion, as well as in most of their customs. So it was with the intention of softening and tempering the stubbornness and harshness of nature that the early Arcadians introduced the practices I have described. Beside this, they inculcated the habit for men and women alike of holding frequent social gatherings, sacrificial ceremonies, and dances performed by young men and girls, and exerted themselves by every possible means to humanize the hardness of the national character through the softening and civilizing influence of such institutions.[32]

Athenaeus confirms the point Polyibus is making.

> But the people of Cynaetha came at the end to neglect these customs [the use of music in education], although they occupied by far the rudest part of Arcadia in point of topography as well as climate; when they plunged right into friction and rivalry with one another they finally became so brutalized that among them alone occurred the gravest acts of sacrilege.[33]

By the end of the period of ancient Greece (beginning ca. 200 BC) the 'Golden Age' was far behind and all hallmarks of society's cultivation were in decline. Accordingly there must have been those who were arguing that the emphasis on using music to develop character in students was no longer valid. Some people were beginning to think of music as mere entertainment and Strabo attacks this philosophy, represented by the Alexandrian writer Eratosthenes (276–194 BC).

> Eratosthenes contends that the aim of every poet is to entertain, not to instruct. The ancients assert, on the contrary, that poetry is a kind of elementary philosophy, which, taking us in our very boyhood, introduces us to the art of life and instructs us, with pleasure to ourselves, in character, emotions, and actions … Why, even the musicians, when they give instruction in singing, in lyre playing, or in aulos playing … maintain that these studies tend to discipline and correct the character.[34]

A discovery in Herculaneum included fragments of a first-century book, 'On Music,' by the Epicurean philosopher, Philodemus of Gadara. The very pretext for writing this book seems to have been a rebuttal to a book by the Stoic philosopher, Diogenes, who had lived a century earlier, and who had contended that the correct use of music, 'will create a disposition which

---

32 Polybius (second century BC), *The Rise of the Roman Empire*, IV, 20.
33 Athenaeus, *Deipnosophistae*, XIV, 626.
34 Strabo, *The Geography of Strabo*, trans. Horace L. Jones (Cambridge: Harvard University Press, 1960), I.2.3.

is harmonious and rhythmic in the highest degree.'[35] While much of Philodemus' commentary on music is rather negative, he was acquainted with the ancient Greek's use of music to form character. His definition of the process includes a divine connection, as we have seen in earlier commentary.

> (They have proposed the theory) that every mode has a Tonos which relates to the emotions assumed to be present [in it]. Melodic composition, rhythms, and the rest are dealt with similarly. Therefore, as they maintain, our inner attitudes become familiarized with the modes in a kind of rapture (literally, 'in the manner of one who is *entheos*,' who has the god within him).[36]

Incidentally, Philodemus quotes an anecdote, for which Diogenes was apparently the source, of a painter who could only capture the correct character of his subject through listening to music as he worked. There is a similar account which has Leonardo da Vinci listening to music while he painted the *Mona Lisa*.

With the beginning of the Christian Era, the Church assumed the role of character formation and officially cast out all the old Greek philosophical ideas about music as being merely 'pagan.' The Church transferred music into the field of mathematics, as far removed from its natural role in communication of feeling as possible. Nevertheless, by the fourth century some Church fathers had begun to adapt the old Greek idea of ethos as part of the ideals of church music. St. Jerome (340–420), for example, observes,

> How the psalm, the hymn, and the song differ one from another we learn most fully in the Psalter. Here let us say briefly that hymns declare the power and majesty of the Lord and continually praise his works and favors, something which all those psalms contain to which the word 'Alleluia' is prefixed or appended. Psalms, moreover, properly affect the seat of the *ethos* in order that by means of this organ of the body we may know what ought to be done and what ought not to be done. The subtle moralist, however, who inquires into these things and examines the harmony of the world and the order and concord of all creatures, sings a spiritual song. To express our opinion more clearly to the simple-minded, the psalm is directed toward the body, the song toward the mind. We ought, then, to sing and to make melody and to praise the Lord more with the heart than with the voice.[37]

By this last sentence, Jerome reflects the official Church position that it is not music itself, but the person, which praises God. Furthermore, it is not the music which is important, but the *words* of the music which one sings.

> Let the servant of Christ sing so that he pleases, not through his voice, but through the words which he pronounces ... [so that one does not] make of the house of God a popular theater.

---

35 Anderson, *Ethos and Education in Greek Music*, 159
36 Ibid., 158.
37 Quoted in Oliver Strunk, *Source Readings in Music History* (New York: Norton, 1950), 72.

St. John Chrysostom (347–407 AD) makes a similar case:

> From strange chants harm, ruin, and many grievous matters are brought in, for those things that are lascivious and vicious in all songs settle in parts of the mind, making it softer and weaker; from the spiritual psalms, however, proceeds music of value, much utility, much sanctity, and every inducement to philosophy, for the words purify the mind....[38]

We have a remarkable discussion of the topic of using music for character formation by Boethius (475–524 AD), a famous mathematician and author of one of the most important medieval treatises on music, *De institutione musica*. Because of the importance of this philosopher still today, we wish to call the reader's attention to four very significant arguments by Boethius.

First, he elevates music above the other liberal arts with respect to its sole role in affecting character ('morality').

Second, he makes the intuitive conclusion that we ourselves are somehow made in the likeness of music. Indeed a group of physicists working with Dr. Hans Jenny in Switzerland have been studying the fact that all our organs produce specific pitches. One of the physicists has concluded that we look as we do as a species due to the combined influence of this internal 'harmony' and gravity.

Three, on the basis of the second idea, it follows that his explanation of how music affects character is solidly based on ancient Greek philosophy, pagan or not.[39]

Four, his conclusion that 'there is no greater ruin of morals in a republic than the gradual perversion of music' requires no better witness than our own time.

Here is the passage in question by Boethius:

> There happen to be four mathematical disciplines [arithmetic, music, geometry, and astronomy], the other three share with music the task of searching for truth; but music is associated not only with speculation but with morality as well. For nothing is more characteristic of human nature than to be soothed by pleasant modes or disturbed by their opposites. This is not peculiar to people in particular endeavors or of particular ages. Indeed, music extends to every endeavor; moreover, youths, as well as the aged are so naturally attuned to musical modes by a kind of voluntary affection that no age at all is excluded from the charm of sweet song. What Plato rightfully said can likewise be understood: the soul of the universe was joined together according to musical concord. For when we hear what is properly and harmoniously united in sound in conjunction with that which is harmoniously coupled and joined together within us and are attracted to it, then we recognize that we ourselves are put together in its likeness. For likeness attracts, whereas unlikeness disgusts and repels.
>
> From this cause, radical transformations in character also arise. A lascivious disposition takes pleasure in more lascivious modes or is often made soft and corrupted upon hearing them. On the other hand, a rougher spirit finds pleasure in more exciting modes or becomes aroused when it hears them. This is the reason why musical modes were named after certain peoples, such as 'Lydian' mode and 'Phrygian,' for in whatever a particular people finds pleasure, by that same name the mode itself is

---

[38] St. John Chrysostom, 'Exposition of Psalm XLI,' quoted in Ibid., 68ff.

[39] His tendency to ignore the positions of the Church had the result, on another occasion, of the pope arranging for his murder.

designated. A people finds pleasure in modes because of likeness to its own character, for it is not possible for gentle things to be joined with or find pleasure in rough things, nor rough things in gentle. Rather, as has been said, similitude brings about love and pleasure. Thus Plato holds that the greatest care should be exercised lest something be altered in music of good character. He states that there is no greater ruin of morals in a republic than the gradual perversion of chaste and temperate music, for the minds of those listening at first acquiesce. Then they gradually submit, preserving no trace of honesty or justice—whether lascivious modes bring something immodest into the dispositions of the people or rougher ones implant something warlike and savage.

> Indeed no path to the mind is as open for instruction as the sense of hearing. Thus, when rhythms and modes reach an intellect through the ears, they doubtless affect and reshape that mind according to their particular character.[40]

He adds that this is exactly what has happened in his own time.

> Since the human race has become lascivious and impressionable, it is taken up totally by representational and theatrical modes. Music was indeed chaste and modest when it was performed on simpler instruments. But since it has been squandered in various, promiscuous ways, it has lost its measure of dignity and virtue; and, having almost fallen into a state of disgrace, it preserves nothing of its ancient splendor.

There are several passing references to the use of music to form character in fourteenth-century Italy, the early Renaissance. Pietro Vergerio, an important humanist and professor of logic in 1391, wrote a treatise, *De ingenuis moribus*, in which he recommends the study of both the theory and practice of music 'as an aid to the inner harmony of the soul.'[41] Vittorino da Feltre (1396–1415), who established a humanistic school in the court of Gianfrancesco Gonzaga in Mantua, was a strong believer in the Greek ideals of music having a beneficial effect on character, and for this purpose he introduced music at meal times for his students.[42] The important music theorist, Marchetto of Padua, unfortunately only mentions the use of music to strengthen the character of the warrior.[43]

Perhaps as a reflection of the music he had heard, one anonymous author from the early fourteenth century finds music can be *harmful* to the character. Although he is relating tales from a much earlier period, we must assume that his choice of these anecdotes reflects to some degree his inclinations.

> Antigonus, the teacher of Alexander [the Great], when one day the latter was having a cythera played for his delight, took hold of the instrument and cast it into the mud, saying 'at your age it behooves you to reign and not to play the cythera. For it may be said that luxury debases the body and the country, as the sound of the cythera enfeebles the soul. Let him then be ashamed who should reign in virtue, and instead delights in luxury.'

---

[40] Boethius, *Fundamentals of Music*, trans. Calvin Bower (New Haven: Yale University Press)

[41] Nan Cooke Carpenter, *Music in the Medieval and Renaissance Universities* (Norman: University of Oklahoma Press, 1958), 40.

[42] Ibid., 44.

[43] Marchetto of Padua, *Lucidarium*, trans. Jan W. Herlinger (Chicago: University of Chicago Press, 1985), I, 3, 5ff.

> King Porrus who fought with Alexander ordered during a banquet that the strings of a player's cythera should be cut, saying, 'it is better to cut than to play, for virtue departs with sweet sounds.'[44]

Another who was bothered by the music he was hearing was Jacques de Liege in Paris. One of the most famous representatives of the *ars antiqua*, he was the author, in about 1313, of *Speculum Musicae*. All art, he contended, must be judged on moral grounds.

> For though art is said to be concerned with what is difficult, it is nevertheless concerned with what is good and useful, since it is a virtue perfecting the soul through the medium of the intellect.[45]

And it was from this perspective that he found 'modern music' (*ars nova*) to be a harmful influence on the character of man.

> For, if I may say so, the old art seems more perfect, more rational, more seemly, freer, simpler, and plainer. Music was originally discreet, seemly, simple, masculine, and of good morals; have not the moderns rendered it lascivious beyond measure?[46]

We might add that another who was unhappy with the music he knew was the fifteenth-century official, Carlo Valgulio (1481–1485), secretary to the papal treasurer and later to Cardinal Cesare Borgia. He also believed that the performance of music was in a general state of decay. In the preface to his translation of Plutarch's 'De musica,' dedicated to the singer Titus Pyrrhinus, he urges the latter to raise the level of performance and its ethical efficacy to that of the ancients.[47] He found that musicians have little regard for these effects, 'filling their books with mere play of notes.'

With the arrival of the High Renaissance we find renewed interest among leading philosophers in the role of music in character formation. The important critic of music, Vincenzo Galilei (1533–1591), began his *Fronimo* by reflecting on his admiration for the views of the ancient civilizations on the virtues of music with respect to character development.

> Music was esteemed to be of such power and virtue by the ancients that it was their opinion that our very souls were harmony, and that sweet and suave harmonies were in this manner inspired to temper uncontrolled emotions so that they should not be discordant with one another. Therefore they took care to introduce good professors of that science, and to honor them with every kind of honor as being useful in their Republics; for the Egyptians never allowed their system of music to be changed by even one note, and just as they had established it, so they continued to accept it for more than ten thousand years, according to their calendar, because they were sure that they could not change the rules and laws of music without serious damage to the body politic.[48]

---

44 'Il Novellino,' trans. Edward Storer (London: Routledge), XIII.

45 Quoted in Strunk, *Source Readings in Music History*, 184.

46 Ibid., 189.

47 Quoted in Claude V. Palisca, *Humanism in Italian Renaissance Musical Thought* (New Haven: Yale University Press, 1985),, 88ff.

48 Vincenzo Galilei, *Fronimo* [1584], trans. Carol MacClintock (Neuhasen-Stuttgart: Hanssler-Verlag, 1985), Preface to the Readers, 27. He was the father to the famous Galileo Galilei.

The sixteenth-century Italian philosopher, Giulio del Bene, also recommended that 'through music we learn to be well ordered and constituted in our minds.'[49]

One of the foremost intellectual influences in Paris in the late Renaissance was the group of poets known as the Pleiade. Their music specialist, Pontus de Tyard, wrote a treatise on music in which he testifies on behalf of the ethical impact of music.

> [Among the ancients] music served as an exercise to temper the soul to a perfect condition of goodness and virtue, exciting and appeasing, by its native power and secret energy, the passions and emotions, as the sounds were carried from the ear to the spiritual parts.[50]

In Germany, Martin Luther also comments on the ability of music to affect the character. He seems to have noticed this first in the quality of people he knew who were also musicians. We may presume that it was his recognition of this purpose of music which fostered his frequent recommendation that music be part of the school curriculum.

> I have always loved music. Those who have mastered this art are made of good stuff, they are fit for any task. It is necessary indeed that music be taught in the schools. A teacher must be able to sing; otherwise I will not as much as look at him. Also, we should not ordain young men into the ministry unless they have become well acquainted with music in the schools.
>
> Music is a beautiful and glorious gift of God and close to theology. I would not give up what little I know about music for something else which I might have in greater abundance. We should always make it a point to habituate youth to enjoy the art of music, for it produces fine and skillful people.[51]

There is an interesting sixteenth-century treatise from England called *Toxophilus*, by Roger Ascham, a tutor to the young Elizabeth I, in which he elaborates on the dangers of music. In this dialog, Toxophilus has been explaining the many virtues of shooting, when Philologus introduces the subject of music by observing that it is a common recreation for scholars. Toxophilus answers by referring to the great purpose of forming the character which one finds in the ancient Greek literature.

> I cannot deny that some music is fit for learning, and I trust you cannot choose but grant that shooting is also fit … But as concerning which of them is most fit for learning and scholars to use, you may say what you will for your pleasure; [but] this I am sure, that Plato and Aristotle … do mention music and all kinds of it; wherein they both agree, that music used amongst the Lydians is very ill for young men which be students for virtue and learning, for a certain nice, soft, and smooth sweetness of it, which would rather entice them to naughtiness than stir them to honesty.

---

49 Quoted in Palisca, *Humanism in Italian Renaissance Musical Thought*, 337.

50 *Solitaire Second ou Discours de la Musique* (Lyons, 1552), quoted in Frances Yates, *The French Academies of the Sixteenth Century* (London: University of London, 1947; Nendeln: Kraus Reprint, 1968), 41.

51 Quoted in Walter Buszin, 'Luther on Music,' *Musical Quarterly* 32, no. 1 (January, 1946): 85, doi: 10.1093/mq/XXXII.1.80

> Another kind of music, invented by the Dorians, they both wonderfully praise, allowing it to be very fit for the study of virtue and learning, because of a manly, rough, and stout sound in it, which should encourage young stomachs to attempt manly matters. Now whether [today's] ballads and rounds, these galliards, pavanes, and dances, so nicely fingered, so sweetly tuned, be more like the music of the Lydians or the Dorians, you may judge for yourself.[52]

Toxophilus then quotes the early physician, Galen, who contended that 'Much music marreth men's manners.' Toxophilus elaborates on this by way of expressing his own worries about the effect of music.

> Although some men will say that it is not so, but rather recreateth and maketh quick a man's mind; yet, methink, by reason it doth as honey doth to a man's stomach, which at the first receiveth it well, but afterward it maketh it unfit to abide any good strong nourishing meat, or else any wholesome sharp and quick drink. And even so in a manner these instruments make a man's wit so soft and smooth, so tender and queasy, that they be less able to brook strong and tough study. Wits be not sharpened, but rather dulled and made blunt, with such sweet softness, even as good edges be blunter which men whet upon soft chalk stones.

Toxophilus then quotes an often repeated anecdote which maintains that Cyrus, after conquering the Lydians and desiring to keep them peaceful, arranged for,

> Every one of them should have a harp or a lute, and learn to play and sing. Which thing if you do … you shall see them quickly of men made women. And thus luting and singing take away a manly stomach, which should enter and pierce deep and hard study.

During the German Baroque we find Johann Mattheson (1681–1764), who was not only a very prolific writer on a wide variety of musical subjects, but an experienced singer, performer on organ and harpsichord and respected composer. For all of Mattheson's pleas that the purpose of music was to move the emotions of the listener, he appears to have been reluctant to go beyond this to the ancient Greek concept of character development. He appears to want to believe that music can change character, and appears to accept the basic logic, but nevertheless he hesitates.

> Plato thought men's habits change with music, namely when it is changed; Cicero maintained however if habits were to change, then music would change. Both can serve our purpose, and neither is wrong. Music and customs should be altered together, so that the former does not damage the latter, nor the latter the former. It is the same with the political …
>
> Besides it is quite regrettable that none of us now knows what constitutes *Musica moralis*. If ethical, or moral philosophy, which concerns the inner man, were only well cultivated; then morals, or ethics which concern the extrinsic, would function better.[53]

---

[52] *Toxophilus*, in *The Whole Works of Roger Ascham*, ed. Rev. Giles (London: John Russell Smith, 1864), II, 25ff.

[53] Johann Mattheson, *Der vollkommene Capellmeister* [1739], trans. Ernest Harriss (Ann Arbor: UMI Research Press, 1981), I, v, 33ff.

Almost as if he is afraid to stand for what he believes, Mattheson lets another speak in his place, quoting the author Lohenstein. Then Mattheson quickly adds, this is 'a statement which can arouse to deeper insight.'[54]

> The eyesight, the sense of smell, the sense of taste and the sense of touch serve the body; but only the sense of hearing is reserved for the soul and our morals.

It is interesting to find, among all the debates on the nature and role of church music during the Baroque, one important composer, Jan Pieters Sweelinck (1562–1621), held an aesthetic of music still firmly rooted in Plato. In a letter to the Burgomasters and Aldermen of Amsterdam of 1603, Sweelinck reflects,

> So great is the correspondence between music and the soul that many, seeking out the essence of the latter, have thought it to be full of harmonious accords, to be, indeed, a pure harmony. All nature itself, to speak the truth, is nothing but a perfect music that the Creator causes to resound in the ears of man, to give him pleasure and to draw him gently to Himself. This we recognize at a glance in the excellent arrangement, the splendid proportions, and the orderly movements and revolutions of the celestial bodies. Therefore some have declared that the Firmament is the original Patron of Music and a true image of the elemental region, as can be observed in the number of elements and their four primary qualities and in the wondrous manner in which their opposites are reconciled.
> This is the reason why the sages of ancient times, considering that each thing has the property of turning, moving, and inclining toward and in accordance with its like, made use of music not only to bring pleasure to the ear, but principally to move and moderate the emotions of the soul. They appropriated it for their oracles in order to gently instill yet firmly incorporate their doctrine into our minds, and thus, having awakened them, could raise them more easily to the contemplation and admiration of the divine.[55]

Among the English philosophers of the Baroque there are some interesting comments on the subject of music's impact on character. Thomas Mace (1613–1709), a very important writer on music theory and criticism, left a discussion of country church music, in which he holds the lack of the use of music in the education of the young to be the cause of his complaints regarding discipline.

> For if [children] be once truly principled in the grounds of piety and music when they are young, they will be like well-seasoned vessels, fit to receive all other good things to be put into them. And I am not only subject to believe, but am very confident, that the vast jarrings, the dischording-untunableness, over-spreading the face of the whole earth, might be much rectified, and put into tune sooner this way, than by any other way that can be thought upon.
> This I speak from an experience in my own soul, who am a man subject to the passions and imperfections of the worst of men. Yet by this virtue, this sublime elixir of musical and harmonical divinity, have found as much (in a comparative way) as this comes to, upon my own soul and violent passions.[56]

---

54 Ibid., I, iii, 26. The source for Lohenstein he gives as *Arminio*, II, 90.

55 Quoted in Gertrude Norman and Miriam Shrifte, *Letters of Composers* (New York, Knopf, 1946), 3.

56 Thomas Mace, *Musick's Monument* [1676] (Paris: Editions du Centre National de la Recherche Scientifique, 1966), 12.

John Milton (1608–1674) is considered by the English to be their greatest poet after Shakespeare. He also makes reference to the ancient Greek assertion that music can change one's character or manners. In the poem 'Arcades,' like Mace, he also attributes to music the ability to raise man above disturbing influences.

> Such sweet compulsion doth in musick lie,
> To lull the daughters of Necessity,
> And keep unsteady Nature to her law,
> And the low world in measured motion draw
> After the heavenly tune, which none can hear
> Of human mold with gross unpurged ear ...[57]

In another poem, 'To Leonora, as She Sings at Rome,' music is referred to as a 'Third Intelligence' which comes from Heaven which enters the throat of the singer and 'graciously teaches mortal hearts the power to grow accustomed insensibly to sounds immortal.'[58]

The purpose of music emphasized by the ancient Greeks, to affect character, is first satirized but then turns serious in a contribution to the fictional 'Memoirs of Scriblerus' by Jonathan Swift (1667–1745).

> The bare mention of music threw Cornelius into a passion. How can you dignify (quoth he) this modern fiddling with the name of Music? Will any of your best Hautboys encounter a wolf now days with no other arms but their instruments, as did that ancient piper Pythocaris? ... Does not Aelian tell us how the Libyan mares were excited to [mating] by Music? (which ought in truth to be a caution to modest women against frequenting Operas; and consider, brother, you are brought to this dilemma, either to give up the virtue of the ladies, or the power of your Music). Whence proceeds the degeneracy of our morals? Is it not from the loss of ancient music, by which (says Aristotle) they taught all the virtues? Else might we turn Newgate [prison] into a college of Dorian musicians, who should teach moral virtues to those people ... It cannot be too often repeated, how the evil spirit departed from Saul, when David played upon his harp.[59] True music being a certain Divine-Magical-Spell, against all diabolical operations in the souls of men. But how little this is taken notice of, believed, or regarded by most, is grievous and lamentable to be thought upon.[60]

In poem by Edward Young (1683–1765) we are closer to the Greek concept of the affect of music on character. Like Martin Luther, he refers to music as the parent of good actions.

> How Music charms! How Meter warms!
> Parent of actions good and brave!
> How Vice it tames, and worth inflames,
> And hold proud empire over the grave![61]

---

57 'Arcades,' in *The Works of John Milton*, ed. Frank Patterson (New York: Columbia University Press, 1931–1938), I, 74.

58 'To Leonora, as She Sings at Rome,' in Ibid., I, 229.

59 I Samuel 16:23, 'And whenever the evil spirit from God was upon Saul, David took the lyre and played it with his hand; so Saul was refreshed and was well and the evil spirit departed from him.'

60 Jonathan Swift is best remembered for *Gulliver's Travels*. He is the best known prose writer at the end of the English Baroque and shared a grandfather with Dryden.

61 Edward Young, 'Ode to the King,' in *Edward Young: The Complete Works* (Hildesheim: Olms, 1968), I, 412.

The foregoing constitutes a remarkable three thousand years of testimony by some of civilization's greatest minds regarding the role of music in forming character. Why, after three thousand years, is this subject no longer discussed? Who is otherwise responsible for the formation of character today?

In American society we have a constitution framed specifically for separating church and state. Thus the church is without influence in the schools. Their influence is limited to the church itself and upon the students who choose to attend. But, as we have seen too often in the news, the church has its own problems with character formation.

The influence of the government is not wanted by the schools, only its money is welcome.

Parents, whose interest in character development should begin with the prenatal period, too often tend to leave the rearing of their children to the schools.

And so, as a last resort, character development falls to the school. If music education can do this its focus must lie in the development of the experiential side of the child. This is the side of the personality where character formation must lie, not on the rational side of the personality. The ancients were right about that. Music education should approach this through a focus on the emotions, in helping the child to come to know himself in that half of his personality. Nothing can do this like music and music teachers, provided only the highest quality classical art music is used.

But professional music educators, shortly after the mid-twentieth century, elected to abandon all prior philosophy and experience in the field of music education. Why?

First, under the fear of 'accountability' music educators have created a system of music education based on 'concepts.' But whatever is 'conceptual' or 'rational' about music, is not music at all. Of course it is easy to grade concepts, but what about the students? Students want the actual experience with music, they want to perform music and learn how to perform music. Students, every last one of them, *love* music even before beginning school. But music educators are not offering what the students are interested in, so the students ignore their classes and go home and teach themselves to sing, to play a keyboard instrument and to compose.

Second, instead of following the ancient advice that only the highest quality music should be used in education, music educators have lowered the quality of the music they use to the lowest common denominator. We regard it as largely a last attempt to make music education more 'popular' with the students.

The past fifty years have also seen a broadening of the repertoire used in the schools to include 'world music.' These exponents say, 'all music is equal.' The great masterpieces of European art music are now just one more choice on the buffet table. Let the student pick whatever he is interested in. But this is like an astronomy teacher placing before the student the completely wrong theories of Ptolemy, Kepler and others in addition to the known scientific facts of today and saying, 'students, pick the theory you like best.' It makes a mockery of the ancient notion that society should pass on to the next generation the best of what it has learned.

What, then, has been the result of American music education over the past fifty years?

Have we created a more sophisticated music culture in America? Or is it becoming lower?

Is music education in the public schools now viewed by the parents and public as being representative of Art or entertainment—or commerce?

Are school music budgets growing larger? Is public support stronger?

Does it matter?

As it turns out, contemporary clinical brain research has proven that musically 'we are what we eat,' that is, our brain is physically changed by the music we listen to. So the ancient philosophers were correct and the music the students hear in school will become part of a permanent record in their minds.

Perhaps music educators in America, if they are observant enough, may rediscover the ancient values in music education by way of the Far East. Shinichi Suzuki has observed,

> Teaching music is not my main purpose. I want to make good citizens.[62]

---

[62] *Reader's Digest*, November, 1973.

On Music and Manners

> *It is true that, as Saint Paul says, every evil word corrupts good manners, but when it has the melody with it, it pierces the heart much more strongly and enters within; as wine is poured into the cask with a funnel, so venom and corruption are distilled to the very depths of the heart by melody.*[1]
>
> John Calvin (1509–1564)

IN ANCIENT TIMES the most frequent advice about controlling the manners of the young involved music. Since music was considered fundamental in establishing character, the subject of the previous essay, the ancients considered a problem in manners to be more on the order of the young person being temporarily 'out of tune' and in need of a musical 'tune up.' Indeed, Vasari, in his *Lives* (of artists) of 1550, uses this very analogy:

> If we bring in music, with its most sweet connections and its very suave intervals, we shall be able to tune, almost like strings, the contrary and diverse motions of our souls.[2]

Italians of this period used the term 'distemper' (literally, to be out of tune) for one who 'is out of tune.' Today we use this term only for mad dogs.

An early biography of Pythagoras (sixth century BC) gave to that philosopher the credit for discovering the power in music to affect manners. Pythagoras, we are told, discovered ancient knowledge,

> which subsists through music's melodies and rhythms, and from these he obtained remedies of human manners and passions, and restored the pristine harmony of the faculties of the soul.[3]

But Athenaeus (ca. 200 AD) maintained that the practice of using music to 'keep in tune' the manners was much more ancient, dating back to the rhapsodists who sung epic poems before the age of written Greek. Singing of the great men of the past at their banquets, according to Athenaeus, enabled the noble guests to restore balance in their character.

> It is plain that Homer observes the ancient Greek system when he says, 'We have satisfied our souls with the equal feast and with the lyre, which the gods have made the companion of the feast,' evidently because the art is beneficial also to those who feast. And this was the accepted custom, it is plain, first in order that every one who felt impelled to get drunk and stuff himself might have music to cure his violence and intemperance, and secondly, because music appeases surliness; for, by stripping off a man's gloominess, it produces good-temper and gladness becoming to a gentleman … It is

---

[1] Jean Calvin, *Geneva Psalter*, quoted in Oliver Strunk, *Source Readings in Music History* (New York: Norton, 1950), 346ff.
[2] Quoted in Claude V. Palisca, *Humanism in Italian Renaissance Musical Thought* (New Haven: Yale University Press, 1985).
[3] Porphyry (ca. 233–305 AD), 'Life of Pythagoras,' trans. Kenneth Guthrie, *The Pythagorean Sourcebook* (Grand Rapids: Phanes Press, 1987).

> plain, therefore, that while most persons devote this art to social gatherings for the sake of correcting conduct and of general usefulness, the ancients went further and included in their customs and laws the singing of praises to the gods by all who attended feasts, in order that our dignity and sobriety might be retained through their help. For, since the songs are sung in concert, if discourse on the gods has been added it dignifies the mood of every one … It is plain, therefore, in the light of what we have said, that music did not, at the beginning, make its way into feasts merely for the sake of shallow and ordinary pleasure, as some persons think.[4]

For a similar purpose, Athenaeus suggests that music was used to keep the manners of wives in place when the husbands went off to war. He cites the *Odyssey*, VIII, 475, in which Agamemnon leaves a rhapsodist behind with Clytaemnestra.

> His business was first to dilate on the virtues of women and inspire emulation for uprightness, and secondly, to furnish pleasant entertainment to divert her mind from low thoughts.[5]

In another place Athenaeus offers his personal observation that 'indeed music trains character, and tames the hot-tempered and those whose opinions clash.'[6]

From the perspective of all early Greek philosophy the key word is the 'soul.' The ancient Greeks often used the analogy of the string instrument, the lyre, to illustrate the relationship of body and soul. One can see the lyre, as a material object like the body, but the sounds it makes are unseen, like the soul. They added to this analogy the word 'harmony,' meaning 'music,' using it to express not only the unity of the various elements of music, but also to express the soul in its ideal state.[7] Plato believed music was given to man by the Gods for this purpose, and not for the more common use of it as entertainment.

> Harmony, which has motions akin to the revolutions of our souls, is not regarded by the intelligent votary of the Muses as given by them with a view to irrational pleasure, which is deemed to be the purpose of it in our day, but as meant to correct any discord which may have arisen in the courses of the soul, and to be our ally in bringing her into harmony and agreement with herself; and rhythm too was given by them for the same reason, on account of the irregular and graceless ways which prevail among mankind generally, and to help us against them.[8]

---

4 Aethenaeus, *Deipnosophistae*, XIV, 627ff.

5 Ibid., I, 14.

6 Ibid., XIV, 623.

7 The first century AD philosopher, Lucretius, in his *On the Nature of the Universe*, III, 126, was tired of hearing the well adjusted quality of man being called 'harmony.'

> Now that we have discovered the nature of the mind and of the vital spirit as part of the man, drop this name harmony which was passed down to the musicians from the heights of Helicon—or else perhaps they fetched it themselves from some other source and applied it to the matter of their art, which had then no name of its own. Whatever it be, let them keep it.

8 *Timaeus*, 47d.

If music was considered this important to education, it stands to reason that someone must oversee the quality of the music itself. Much as Plato would recommend later for his utopian city, Plutarch (46–122 AD) suggests that the music and sung poetry used in education was subject to civic censors.

> They adjudged it necessary for the preservation of that gravity and seriousness of manners which was required of their youth for the attainments of wisdom and virtue, never to admit of any light and wanton, any ludicrous or effeminate poetry; which made them allow of no poets among them but such only who for their grave and virtuous compositions were approved by the public magistrate; that being hereby under some restraint, they might neither act nor write any thing to the prejudice of good manners, or to the dishonor of their laws and government.[9]

The power of music to change behavior and manners was also remarked on by the ancient Romans. Since the quality of the music was an important key to the effectiveness of music changing manners, the philosopher, Quintilian (30–96 AD) began his discussion by commenting on the deterioration of music in his time.

> I think I ought to be more emphatic than I have been in stating that the music which I desire to see taught is not our modern music, which has been emasculated by the lascivious melodies of our effeminate stage and has to no small extent destroyed such manly vigor as we still possessed. No, I refer to the music of old which was employed to sing the praises of brave men and was sung by the brave themselves. I will have none of your psalteries and viols, that are unfit even for the use of a modest girl.

Then he addressed the power of music to affect manners by retelling a story told about Pythagoras. Included here is a very rare reference to a female aulos player.

> Give me the knowledge of the principles of music, which have power to excite or assuage the emotions of mankind. We are told that Pythagoras on one occasion, when some young men were led astray by their passions to commit an outrage on a respectable family, calmed them by ordering the aulos player to change her strain to a spondaic meter.

He follows this with a rather extraordinary illustration, although he doubts it is true.

> Further I may point out that among the fictitious themes employed in declamation is one, doing no little credit to its author's learning, in which it is supposed that an aulos player is accused of manslaughter because he had played a tune in the Phrygian mode as an accompaniment to a sacrifice, with the result that the person officiating went mad and flung himself over a precipice.[10]

A later Roman philosopher, Sextus Empiricus (second century AD), who was often negative in general toward music, makes an observation regarding the above story about Pythagoras.

---

9   'Customs of the Lacedaemonians.'

10 Quintilian, *The Education of an Orator* (*Institutio Oratoria*), trans. H. E. Butler (London: Heinemann, 1938),

> As to Pythagoras, in the first place he was foolish in desiring to render drunkards sober at the wrong moment, instead of quitting the place; and secondly, by trying to reform them in this way he confesses that aulos players have more influence than philosophers for the reforming of morals.[11]

Empiricus, himself, concluded that there is no evidence that music leads one either to wisdom or virtue. Indeed, he believed, music often has the effect of 'making young people easily led into incontinence and debauchery.'

With the arrival of the Christian Era we find a comment by one of the church fathers, Clement of Alexandria (ca. 150–215 AD), which also mentions the ancient banquet tradition. Here he specifically speaks of the use of music to improve manners and emphasizes the importance of using only good music for this purpose.

> Music is then to be handled for the sake of the embellishment and composure of manners. For instance, at a banquet we pledge each other while the music is playing; soothing by song the eagerness of our desires, and glorifying God for the copious gift of human enjoyments, for His perpetual supply of the food necessary for the growth of the body and of the soul. But we must reject superfluous music, which enervates men's souls, and leads to variety,—now mournful, and then licentious and voluptuous, and then frenzied and frantic.[12]

Martianus Capella, of whom little is known, composed in the middle of the fifth century a remarkable allegorical work describing a heavenly wedding called 'The Marriage of Mercury and Philology,' or the Marriage of Eloquence and Learning, in which the seven bridegrooms were the seven disciplines of the liberal arts and the guests were various Greek gods, together with a dozen famous earlier philosophers. In this work he speaks of the power to change manners and behavior.

> When an unruly mob of common people were raging at the city fathers as they were deliberating, the sound of music that rose above their obstreperous clamor held them in check. Some young men in a drunken condition who were behaving in a rowdy manner were brought to their senses by the musicianship of Damon, one of my disciples. He ordered them to sing some spondaic measures to the accompaniment of a aulos, and brought their noisy brawling to an abrupt halt.[13]

We have an extraordinary survey of the aesthetics of music by Cassiodorus (480–573 AD) in a letter to the famous Boethius. His purpose in writing was to ask Boethius to find a harp player to fulfill a request by Clovis, king of the Franks, whom Cassiodorus suggests has 'heard of the fame of my banquets.' He requests Boethius to find someone 'who is skilled in musical knowledge,' who with his 'sweet sound can tame the savage hearts of the barbarians.' In this letter he mentions the power of music to affect manners.

---

[11] Sextus Empiricus, 'Against the Musicians,' in *Against the Professors*, trans. R. G. Bury (Cambridge: Harvard University Press, 1949), VI, 19ff.

[12] Clement of Alexandria, in 'The Miscellanies,' trans. William Wilson (Edinburgh: T. & T. Clark, 1884), Book VI, xi.

[13] *Martianus Capella and the Seven Liberal Arts*, trans. William Harris Stahl and Richard Johnson (New York: Columbia University Press, 1977), 358.

> The artist changes men's hearts as they listen; and, when this artful pleasure issues from the secret place of nature as the queen of the senses, in all the glory of its tones, our remaining thoughts take to flight, and it expels all else, that it may delight itself simply in being heard. Harmful melancholy he turns to pleasure; he weakens swelling rage; he makes bloodthirsty cruelty kindly, arouses sleepy sloth from its torpor, restores to the sleepless their wholesome rest, recalls lust-corrupted chastity to its moral resolve, and heals boredom of spirit which is always the enemy of good thoughts. Dangerous hatreds he turns to helpful goodwill, and, in a blessed kind of healing, drives out the passions of the heart by means of sweetest pleasures.

Later in this same letter, Cassiodorus briefly mentions the effect of the music on various peoples in accomplishing this.

> The Dorian mode bestows wise self-restraint and establishes chastity; the Phrygian arouses strife, and inflames the will to anger; the Aeolian calms the storms of the soul, and gives sleep to those who are already at peace; the Ionian sharpens the wits of the dull, and, as a worker of good, gratifies the longing for heavenly things among those who are burdened by earthly desire. The Lydian was discovered as a remedy for excessive cares and weariness of the spirit: it restores it by relaxation, and refreshes it by pleasure.[14]

Guido of Arezzo, in his important music treatise, *Micrologus* of ca. 1026–1028 AD, provides an illustration of the ability of music to affect behavior in an anecdote not found elsewhere. As to the explanation how music does this, he cannot say, offering only the observation that this is known only to Divine Wisdom.

> Another man was roused by the sound of the cithara to such lust that, in his madness, he sought to break into the bedchamber of a girl, but, when the cithara player quickly changed the mode, was brought to feel remorse for his libidinousness and to retreat abashed.[15]

The thirteenth-century philosopher, Bartholomew Anglicus, writes that it belongs to the very power of music to bring about changes in men.

> Also by sweet songs of harmony and accord of music, sick men and frantic come oft to their wit again and health of body. Some men tell that Orpheus said,
> *Emperors pray me to feasts, to have liking of me; but I have liking of them which would bend their hearts from wrath to mildness, from sorrow to gladness, from covetousness to largeness, from dread to boldness.*[16]

Johannes de Grocheo, began his music treatise, *De Musica* (ca. 1300), not with the usual definition of music, but rather with a defense of why music is important.

14　Letter to Boethius, in *Variae*, trans. Thomas Hodgkin (London: Frowde, 1886)., II, xl.
15　Hucbald, 'Melodic Instruction' in *Hucbald, Guido, and John on Music*, trans. Warren Babb (New Haven: Yale University Press, 1978), 160.
16　Quoted in *Medieval Lore*, trans. Robert Steele (London: Stock, 1893), 64.

> An understanding of music is necessary to those who wish to have a complete understanding of bodies moving and moved ... It is also good in a practical sense, for it corrects and improves the customs of men if used in the proper way.[17]

Marsilio Ficino, the fifteenth-century founder of the Florentine Academy, was a philosopher who was an active musician in his leisure, playing the lyre for his own relaxation, but also in concerts in the Medici palace.[18] Music, he believed, served man's 'spirit' in the same way medicine serves the body and theology the soul. The music one hears provokes a memory in the soul of the divine music found in the mind of God and in the music of the spheres.[19] Through affecting the spirit, music also affects the body and soul. He says he personally found music valuable for ridding the body of disturbances and lifting his mind to a higher level of intellect.[20] His contemporary, Franchino Gaffurio, in his 'Theorica musice,' also stresses the ethical potential of music.

> Socrates and Plato and also the Pythagoreans, attributing a moral resource to music, ordered by a common law that adolescents and youth, and young women too, be educated in music, not for inciting to desire, through which this discipline becomes cheapened, but for moderating the movements of the soul through rule and reason.[21]

Desideratum Erasmus (1469–1536) was the greatest humanist, scholar and writer of prose of the early sixteenth century in the Low Countries. In a lengthy letter to Pope Adrian VI in 1522, Erasmus writes of the power of music to change behavior and retells the story about Pythagoras.

> It is a property, they say, of man-made music that it can either rouse the emotions or control them if a skilled performer makes an appropriate use of specific harmonies. It is said that Timotheus could kindle the heart of Alexander of Macedon with warlike fire by playing in certain particular modes. Pythagoras, by playing spondees in the Phrygian mode, transformed a young man mad with love and restored his sanity. A similar story is told of Empedocles, who is said by the use of some particular musical modes to have recalled to his proper wits a young man already beside himself with rage and hell-bent on murder. The tales told in antiquity of Mercury and Orpheus playing on the lyre look like fables; and yet these fictions were inspired by the wonders music can perform.

Since the ancient writers had placed great emphasis on using only good music when matters of character were involved, Erasmus, in another place, writes at length on the dangers to the morals of young women of the vulgar popular music of his time.

---

[17] Johannes de Garlandia, *De Mensurabili Musica*, trans. Stanley Birnbaum (Colorado Springs: Colorado Collge Music Press, 1978), 1.

[18] Paul Kristeller, 'Music and Learning in the Early Italian Renaissance,' *The Journal of Renaissance and Baroque Music* 1, no. 4 (June 1947): 269ff, http://www.jstor.org/stable/20528744

[19] Ficino carries his belief in the 'music of the spheres' to an association of the signs of the zodiac with the tones of the scale.

[20] Quoted in Nino Pirrotta, 'Music and Cultural Tendencies in fifteenth-Century Italy,' *Journal of the American Musicological Society* 19, no. 2 (1966): 140, http://www.jstor.org/stable/830579

[21] Quoted in Claude V. Palisca, *Humanism in Italian Renaissance Musical Thought*, 193.

> It is customary now among some nations to compose every year new songs which young girls study assiduously. The subject matter of the songs is usually the following: a husband deceived by his wife, or a daughter guarded in vain by her parents, or a clandestine affair of lovers. These things are presented as if they were wholesome deeds, and a successful act of profligacy is applauded. Added to pernicious subject matter are such obscene innuendoes, expressed in metaphors and allegories, that no manner of depravity could be depicted more vilely.
>
> Many earn a livelihood in this occupation, especially among the Flemish. If laws were enforced, composers of such common ditties would be flogged for singing these doleful songs to the licentious. Men who publicly corrupt youth are making a living from crime, yet parents are found who think it a mark of good breeding if their daughters know such songs.
>
> Antiquity considered music to belong to the liberal disciplines. Since musical sounds have great power to affect the soul of man…the ancients carefully distinguished musical modes, preferring the Dorian to others. They believed this matter to be so important that laws were enacted so that music would not be permitted in the state if it corrupted the minds of citizens.
>
> But in our music, apart from obscenity in texts and subjects, how much is frivolity, how much is folly? There existed in former times a kind of performance in which, without words and only by pantomime, anything that was desired could be represented. In the same way in modern songs, even if the text is not sung, the foulness of the subject can be understood from the nature of the music. Then add to this the sound of frenetic pipes and noisy drums combining with a frenzy of movements. To such music young girls dance, to this they are accustomed, and yet we think there is no danger to their morals.[22]

The important English Church philosopher, Richard Hooker (1553–1600), a rational voice which attempted to counter the radical Puritans, shared the concern of Erasmus for the influence of vulgar music.

> In [music] the very image and character even of virtue and vice is perceived, the mind delighted with their resemblances, and brought by having them often iterated into a love of the things themselves. For which cause there is nothing more contagious and pestilent than some kinds of [music]; then some nothing more strong and potent unto good. And that there is such a difference of one kind from another we need no proof but our own experience.[23]

The greatest French writer of the sixteenth century was unquestionably Michel Montaigne (1533–1592). After an education in law at Toulouse, he became in turn a soldier, courtier, traveler and mayor of Bordeaux. In one of his famous essays he observes,

> No heart is … so hard that sweet music does not tickle it and enliven it; no soul is so sour that it does not feel touched by some feeling of reverence when it … hears the enchantment of the organ and the poised religious harmony of men's voices.[24]

---

[22] Erasmus, *Opera omnia*, ed. J. Clericus (Leiden, 1703–1706), V, 717F, quoted in Clement A. Miller, 'Erasmus on Music,' in *The Musical Quarterly* 52, no. 3 (July, 1966): 347ff, http://www.jstor.org/stable/3085961.

[23] Richard Hooker, *On the Laws of Ecclesiastical Polity*, V, xxxviii, in *The Works of Mr. Richard Hooker* (Oxford: Clarendon Press, 1888), II, 159.

[24] Michel de Montaigne, *Essays*, trans. M. A. Screech (London: Penguin, 1993), II, xii, 670

He adds, unfortunately without elaboration, that he knows some doctors who maintain that people with certain complexions can be driven mad by certain sounds or instruments.

At about this time in France, Charles IX, in a patent document relative to Baif's Academy, noted that,

> it is of great importance for the morals of the citizens of a town that the music current and used in the country should be retained under certain laws, for the minds of most men are formed and their behavior influenced by its character, so that where music is disordered, there morals are also depraved, and where it is well ordered, there men are well disciplined morally.[25]

When the revival of drama began in the Renaissance, drama followed music in adding an educational purpose to its art. Sebastiano, known as Minturno, was bishop of Ugento, and represented that town in the council of Trent. Author of two books on drama criticism, *Arte Poetica* (1563, in Italian) and a *De Poeta* (1559, in Latin), he emphasizes that 'the ennobling or purification of manners is the end toward which all effort is directed.'[26]

Juan Vives, author of a famous sixteenth-century book, *On Education*, continues in the Church Scholastic tradition of classifying music as a branch of mathematics. However, whereas he finds geometry and arithmetic as vital instruments for the search of Truth, he assigns music a lesser value, 'for relaxation and recreation of the mind through the harmony of sounds.'[27] Interestingly enough, he still classifies all poetry under the heading of music.

When discussing the appropriate subject matter for schools, Vives again defines music as 'arithmetic applied to sounds' and all the mathematical sciences, including music, have two aspects, the contemplative or theoretical and the practical.[28]

Philologists believe that we all carry as a gift from early man the lyric contours of our spoken sentences. Vives seems to have been aware of an early source, unknown to us, which suggested this effect was even stronger in ancient times.

> In music we have deteriorated much from the older masters, on account of the dullness of the ear which has utterly lost all discrimination of subtle sounds, so that now we no longer distinguish even the long and short sounds in common speech; and for this reason we have lost some kinds of meters, and that primitive harmony of tones, the effects of which the ancient writers testify were vast and marvelous.[29]

Vives contends that music should be part of education for the purpose of stabilizing the students' manners and he specifies the importance of using only good music.

---

[25] Quoted in Frances Yates, *The French Academies of the Sixteenth Century* (London: University of London, 1947; Nendeln: Kraus Reprint, 1968), 23.

[26] Barrett Clark, *European Theories of the Drama* (New York: Crown, 1959), 58ff.

[27] *Vives: On Education*, trans. Foster Watson (Cambridge: University Press, 1913), I, v.

[28] Ibid., IV, v.

[29] Ibid.

> Only let the pupil practice pure and good music which, after the Pythagorean mode, soothes, recreates, and restores to itself the wearied mind of the student; then let it lead back to tranquility and tractability all the wild and fierce parts of the student's nature.[30]

In sixteenth-century Germany we find an interesting early work by Henry Agrippa, his *De occulta philosophia*. Here, in a chapter entitled, 'Of Musical Harmony, of the Force and Power thereof,' he begins by observing that,

> Musical harmony also is not destitute of the gifts of the stars; for it is a most powerful imaginer of all things, which whilst it follows opportunely the celestial bodies, doth wonderfully allure the celestial influence, and doth change the affections, intentions, gestures, motions, actions, and dispositions of all the hearers, and doth quietly allure them to its own properties, as to gladness, lamentation, to boldness, or rest, and the like.[31]

Martin Luther is reported to have mentioned this purpose in a dinner conversation.

> Music is a semi-discipline and taskmistress, which makes people milder and more gentle, more civil and more sensible.[32]

We also find some interesting comments on our subject in sixteenth-century German music treatises. Andreas Ornithoparchus, author of *Musice active micrologus* of 1517, was associated with several universities, in particular Leipzig and Tubingen. The very purpose of his book, he announces, is to provide the youth of all of Germany with a book which would introduce them to good fashions, the honest delights of music and 'little by little stir them to virtuous actions.' In this, he continues,

> Among those things by which the mind of man is wont to be delighted, I can find nothing that is more great, that appeals to any age or sex ... There is no breast so savage and cruel, which is not moved with the touch of this delight. For it drives away cares, persuades men to gentleness, represses anger, nourishes arts, promotes concord, inflames heroic minds to gallant deeds, cures vice, breeds virtues and nourishes them ... Therefore this Art is of a holy, sweet, heavenly, divine, fair and blessed nature.[33]

Ornithoparchus returns to this subject again at the end of Book I when he discusses the character of the various medieval Church modes. Dorian, he says, bestows wisdom to and causes chastity in the listener, while Phrygian causes wars and inflames fury. Aeolian calms the tempest of the mind and, after having done so, lulls it to sleep. Lydian sharpens the wit of the

---

[30] Ibid.

[31] Henry Cornelius Agrippa, *De occulta Philosophia*, II, xxiv. The best modern edition, which is highly recommended, is Donald Tyson, *Three Books of Occult Philosophy* (St. Paul: Llewellyn Publications, 1993).

[32] Quoted in Walter Buszin, 'Luther on Music,' *The Musical Quarterly* 32, no. 1 (January, 1946): 92, http://www.jstor.org/stable/739566.

[33] Ornithoparchus, *Musicae active mirologus and Dowland, Introduction: Containing the Art of Singing* (New York: Dover, 1973), 117ff.

dull and moves the mind from earthly to heavenly desires. No wonder Ornithoparchus warns that the musician must diligently observe which mode he plays for specific listeners! The men of our time, he says, know how to do this according to the nature of the occasion.

> And that is not without cause, for every habit of the mind is governed by songs. For songs make men sleepy and wakeful, careful and merry, angry and merciful. Songs heal diseases and produce diverse wonderful effects, moving some to vain mirth, some to a devout and holy joy, yes often to godly tears.

At the beginning of Book II, Ornithoparchus mentions the Roman emperor Nero as an illustration of how a man is affected by music.

> Even Nero, while he gave himself to music, was most gentle. But when he abandoned music in favor of the diabolical Art of Necromancy, then first appeared that fierce cruelty of his. Then he was changed from a lamb into a wolf and from a most mild prince into a most savage beast.

Nicolaus Listenius (ca. 1500–1550), the author of *Musica*, of 1537, matriculated at Wittenberg in 1529 when both Luther and Melancthon were teaching there. This book is dedicated to Johann Georg, son of Joachim II, the elector of Brandenburg, and it seems rather daring to us when Listenius tells the prince that by cultivating music he will be worthy of his ancestors. In this same Foreword, Listenius writes of the impact on manners of music, this 'serious art.'

> Many great and serious reasons are established by learned and intelligent men, for all men of genius particularly free princes, must be versed in music and habituated to it. It influences souls to humanity, suavity, even-temper; it restrains all immoderate affections, grief, wrath; it represses violence and obscene desires, for it calms them; as in sounds and songs, so in all the actions of life we may conserve harmony. Hence we see the highest kings in old monuments singing and playing on strings, not only as a pastime for the enjoyment of the arts, but even more, however, making it a serious art, tying music to the harmony of the soul …
> This art invites the soul to virtue.[34]

On the other hand, there are two English books written in the sixteenth century which are suspicious of, if not opposed to, the ancient idea that music can improve manners. Roger Ascham (1515–1568), a tutor to the young Elizabeth I, in his *The Schoolmaster* (1570), seems particularly concerned that *too* much study is bad for a man. He has observed that 'those which be commonly the wisest, the best learned, and best men' when young, seem to lose their 'quickest of wit' when older. The explanation, he believes, must be something like a sharp knife which becomes dull.[35] It follows, according to Ascham, that there is a danger in extended study and, indeed, he specifically points to the ill effects on manners by the extended study of music.

---

34 Nicolaus Listenius, *Musica*, trans. Albert Seay (Colorado Springs: Colorado College Music Press, 1975), 1.

35 Roger Ascham, *The Schoolmaster* [1570], ed. Lawrence Ryan (Ithaca: Cornell University Press, 1967), 21ff.

> Some wits, moderate enough by nature, be many times marred by overmuch study and use of some sciences, namely, music, arithmetic and geometry. These sciences, as they sharpen men's wits overmuch, so they change men's manners oversore, if they be not moderately mingled and wisely applied to some good use of life.

He quotes, in support of his view, the early medical writer, Galen (second century AD), as saying 'Much music marreth men's manners.' Ascham then concludes, with a reference to manners, that 'overmuch quickness of wit,' whether by nature or by study, does not result in the 'greatest learning, best manners, or happiest life.'

Lodowick Bryskett (1546–1612), in his *A Discourse of Civill Life*, begins with a review of a number of ancient Greek philosophers and their philosophies and provides an extensive summary of other purposes and virtues of music.[36] He agrees that the kind of music we *should* have is found in the writings of the ancient Greeks. It should be grave, with learned and grave verses by excellent poets, and should create magnificent and noble desires in the minds of the listeners. Such music enters,

> like lively sparks into men's minds, to kindle in them desires of dignity, greatness, honor, true praise and commendation, and to correct whatsoever is in them of base and vile affection.[37]

His concern is that because of the deterioration of music in his time (Elizabethan music!), the ancient principle of the use of music to improve manners may no longer be valid. Young men today, he advises, must be very selective of what they listen to.

> Let it suffice that young men are to take great account of that part of music which bears with it grave melodies, fit to compose the mind to good order by virtue of the rhythms and sound ... But those which by variety in tunes, and warbling variations, confounds the words and melodies, and yields only a delight to the exterior sense, and no fruit for the mind, I wish them to neglect and not to esteem.
>
> Indeed ... our music is far different from the ancient music and while it may well serve to please the ear, I say that it 'effeminateth' the mind and diverts it from bliss and felicity.[38]

Sixteenth-century nobles, especially in Italy, felt that after a dinner party, during which there was much debating and arguing, it was important to conclude the evening by singing in order to bring everyone into 'harmony.' We find it somewhat charming, therefore, that the Baroque German composer, Johann Kuhnau, seems to turn this argument around, suggesting that the harmony of the music teaches men how to speak in a harmonious fashion.

---

[36] Lodowick Bryskett, *A Discourse of Civill Life*, ed. Thomas Wright (Northridge: San Fernando Valley State College, 1970), 107ff. We have converted this to modern English. Bryskett (1546–1612) functioned as a secretary to a variety of English politicians.

[37] Ibid., 146.

[38] Ibid., 113.

> The musicians in cities commonly hold a collegium musicum every week or two. That is indeed a laudable undertaking, in part because it provides them with the opportunity to refine further their excellent art, and in part, too, because they learn from the pleasing harmonies how to speak together concordantly, even though these same people mostly disagree with one another at other times.[39]

Marin Mersenne (1588–1648), author of the great French *Harmonie universelle* of 1636, was thinking along these lines. He wonders, for example, why man was made with the ability to make only one sound at a time.[40] He doubts that man would be able to accomplish anything he cannot do with one voice and concludes that God made it necessary for man to need another man to make harmony, 'so that the harmony of voices might invite men to the harmony of manners.'[41]

However, in a letter to Huygens, he privately confessed doubt whether music can in fact have as significant influence on the actions of man as a good sermon.

> For to think that music serves to persuade us of the intention of the musician as perfectly as could a good orator, and that it has as much power to conduct us to virtue and to make us hate vice as much as the voice of a good preacher, even though the same things are sung as he recites in the pulpit, and to believe that singing can be used as easily for instruction as can speaking and lecturing, it is this that it is difficult for us to accept.[42]

There was somewhat more discussion of the ability of music to affect manners in England during the Baroque. Thomas Mace (1613–1709) laments the loss of the music of former times, specifically the consort music of the early seventeenth century.

> We had for our grave music, Fancies of 2, 3, 5, and 6 parts to the organ; interposed (now and then) with some pavans, allmaines, solemn, and sweet delightful ayres; all of which (as it were) so many Pathetical Stories, Rhetorical and sublime discourses; subtle, and acute argumentations, so suitable, and agreeing to the inward, secret, and intellectual faculties of the soul and mind; that so set them forth according to their true praise, there are no words sufficient in language; yet what I can best speak of them, shall be only to say, that they have been to myself (and many others), as divine raptures, powerfully captivating all our unruly faculties, and affections (for the time) and disposing us to Solidity, Gravity, and Good Temper, making us capable of Heavenly, and Divine influences.
> It is a great pity few believe thus much; but far greater, that so few know it.[43]

The fashion today, he notes, has replaced these things with an emphasis on the virtuoso performer, 'the Great Idol,' and music,

---

39 Johann Kuhnau, *Der musicalische Quack-Salber* [Dresden, 1700], Chapter I. Kuhnau (1660–1722), like Bach, was the music director of St. Thomas in Leipzig. Although known today as a composer, he was educated in law and mathematics and was capable in Hebrew, Greek and Latin.

40 Marin Mersenne, *Harmonie universelle* [1636], III, i, 21. In III, i, 22, Mersenne mentions that the 'son of Pierre d'Avignon' astonished everyone by singing one part and whistling another simultaneously.

41 Ibid., III, i, 6.

42 Letter to Constantin Huygens, November 14, 1640.

43 Thomas Mace, *Musick's Monument* [1676] (Paris: Editions du Centre National de la Recherche Scientifique, 1966), 234.

which is rather fit to make a man's ears glow, and fill his brains full of frisks, etc., than to season, and sober his mind, or elevate his affection to Goodness.

The first great philosopher of the English Baroque was Francis Bacon (1561–1626). In his *Natural History* he devotes a lengthy discussion of the role of music in affecting manners and attempts to explain how it works.

> It has been anciently held and observed, that the sense of hearing and the kinds of music most in operation upon manners; as to encourage men and make them warlike; to make them soft and effeminate; to make them grave; to make them light; to make them gentle and inclined to pity; etc. The cause is, for that the sense of hearing strikes the spirits more immediately than the other senses, and more incorporeally than the smelling. For the sight, taste, and feeling, have their organs not of so present and immediate access to the spirits, as the hearing has. And as for the smelling (which indeed works also immediately upon the spirits, and is forcible while the object remains), it is with a communication of the breath or vapor of the object odorate; but harmony, entering easily, and mingling not at all, and coming with a manifest motion, doth by custom of often affecting the spirits and putting them into one kind of posture, alter not a little the nature of the spirits, even when the object is removed. And therefore we see that tunes and airs, even in their own nature, have in themselves some affinity with the affections: as there be merry tunes, doleful tunes, solemn tunes; tunes inclining men's minds to pity; warlike tunes, etc. So as it is no marvel if they alter the spirits, considering that tunes have a predisposition to the motion of the spirits in themselves. But yet it hath been noted, that though this variety of tunes disposes the spirits to variety of passions conform unto them, yet generally music feeds that disposition of the spirits which it finds. We see also that several airs and tunes do please several nations and persons, according to the sympathy they have with their spirits.[44]

John Milton (1608–1674) is considered by the English to be their greatest poet after Shakespeare. In his treatise, 'On Education,' he recommends music for the student's periods of rest, for education in manners and to temper the passions. The reader will also notice that Milton stresses the importance of using only good music for this purpose.

> The interim of unsweating themselves regularly, and convenient rest before meat may both with profit and delight be taken up in recreating and composing their travailed spirits with the solemn and divine harmonies of Musick heard or learned; either while the skillful organist plies his grave and fancied descant, in lofty fugues, or the whole Symphony with artful and unimaginable touches adorn and grace the well studied chords of some choice Composer; sometimes the Lute, or soft Organ stop waiting on elegant Voices either to Religious, martial, or civil verses; which if wise men and Prophets be not extremely out, have a great power over the dispositions and manners, to smooth and make them gentle from rustic harshness and distempered passions. The like also would not be unexpedient after Meat to assist and cherish Nature in her first concoction, and send their minds back to study in good tune and satisfaction.[45]

---

[44] *Natural History*, Section 114, in *The Works of Francis Bacon*, ed. James Spedding (Cambridge: Cambridge University Press, 1869).

[45] 'On Education,' in *The Works of John Milton*, ed. Frank Patterson (New York: Columbia University Press, 1931–1938), IV, 288ff.

Joseph Addison, writing in the *Spectator* for 14 June 1712, briefly reviews the use of music in the Old Testament and in the religious rites of the ancient Greeks, after which he wishes,

> Had we frequent entertainments of this nature among us, they would not a little purify and exalt our passions, give our thoughts a proper turn, and cherish those divine impulses in the soul, which every one feels that has not stifled them by sensual and immoderate pleasures.
>
> Musick, when thus applied, raises noble hints in the mind of the hearer, and fills it with great conceptions. It strengthens devotion, and advances praise into rapture.

We find this topic discussed by one of the nineteenth century's great composers *and* philosophers, Richard Wagner. His discussion is not limited to the individual, but entire societies.

> No less than Drama, Music is able to work on taste, yes, also on *manners*: the first point will be disputed by no one, even in our day; but a direct relation to morality has not as yet been generally ascribed to Music, in fact it has even been judged as morally quite harmless.
>
> This is not so. Could an effeminate and frivolous taste remain without influence on a man's morality? Both go hand in hand, and act reciprocally upon each other: not to refer to the Spartans, who forbade a certain type of music as injurious to morals,—let us think back to our own immediate past; with tolerable certainty we may contend that those inspired by Beethoven's music must have been more active and energetic citizens of the State than those bewitched by Rossini, Bellini and Donizetti, a class consisting for the most part of rich and lordly do-nothings. A speaking proof is further afforded by Paris: anyone might have observed during the last decades that in exact degree as the morals of Parisian society have rushed into that unexampled corruption, its music has floundered in a sphere of frivolous taste; one has only to hear the latest compositions of an Auber, Adam and so on, and to compare them with the odious dances performed in Paris at the time of Carnival, to perceive a terrible connection. If this rather proves that Morals operate on Music, yet the mutual relation of the two is manifest; it consequently is the State's affair to apply to this art, as well, that demand addressed by Kaiser Joseph to the theater: 'that it shall work for the ennobling of taste *and* manners.'[46]

Now *there* is a nice line by Franz Joseph! Wouldn't it be nice if music education took that line as *its* mission statement?

Music education shall work for the ennobling of taste *and* manners.

While the early philosophers, for two thousand years blamed decay in music for any decay in manners, Wagner raised the opposite question. Indeed one often reads, in art criticism, that 'art reflects life.' This seems a valid question relative to the music the public listens to in our time. Certainly it must be recognized that the popular music has become so degenerate as to have been unimaginable in earlier times. But is this vulgar music only reflecting society, or has society allowed this music to diminish society itself?

Who is there to speak out on the subject of the vulgar popular music of today? Certainly not most music educators, even though they should be society's experts. Is there a university professor anywhere who is concerned about rap? If you have ever wondered what you are

---

[46] Quoted in *Wagner's Prose Works*, trans. William Ashton Ellis (New York: Broude), VII, 355ff.

hearing when you hear rap, here is a translation by an Oakland High School student of a song from the album 'Ready to Die,' by the Notorious B.I.G. This is what your children are listening to, and they, unlike you, understand it.

Lyrics:
First things first, I poppa, freaks all the honeys
Dummies–playboy bunnies, those wantin' money
Those the ones I like 'cause they don't get nathan'
But penetration, unless it smells like sanitation
Garbage, I turn like doorknobs
Heart throb, never, black and ugly as ever
However, I stay coochied down to the socks
Rings and watch filled with rocks

Translation:
As a general rule, I perform deviant sexual acts with women of all kinds, including but not limited to those with limited intellect, nude magazine models, and prostitutes. I particularly enjoy sexual encounters with the latter group as they are generally disappointed in the fact that they only receive penile intercourse and nothing more, unless of course, they douche on a consistent basis. Although I am extremely unattractive, I am able to engage in these types of sexual acts with some regularity. Perhaps my sexuality is somehow related to my fancy and expensive jewelry.[47]

---

[47] http://72.14.203.104/search?q=cache:CkV6w1rf5RgJ:www.bizbag.com/Misc%2520article....

On the Character of the Performer

> *How can a man tune a lute who is himself out of tune?*
> *What sense of harmony can he have who is himself full of discords?*
>
> Fernando de Rojas (1477–1541)
>
> *A chaste poet will produce chaste poems.*
>
> Cervantes (1547–1616)

WE, AS HUMANS, HAVE TWO SIDES. We have a rational side, for the most part the left hemisphere of the brain, which is an accumulation of a life time exposure to data: the English, or some other language; math; books and newspapers, etc. But none of this is *us*, it is all something we have been told by someone else. The other side of our self, for the most part the right hemisphere of the brain, is the *real us*, for it consists of what we have learned from our own direct, personal experience.

In most professions the *real* person is hidden from view. A physician, for example, deals in a world of facts and everything he does or says is based on rational information. We never see the *real* person. The same is true of an actor. He is representing a character in a script, a fictional character consisting of words. The good actor *becomes* this fictional character on stage, but we do not see the *real* actor.

Only in a musician is it possible to see the *real* person. When we look at a painting by Van Gogh we do not immediately communicate with Van Gogh, for the canvas stands between us. We must deal with the canvas by eye before we can hope to see what the artist was thinking. Music is quite different. Music is the only art in which the observer (listener) has a direct connection with the artist (composer). This is because of the universal and genetic nature of emotions, the language of music. When a performer performs a Beethoven piano sonata the performer must personify the emotions of Beethoven. Beethoven is dead. The only way Beethoven can come alive is through the emotions and feelings of the performer. At the same time, again because of the universal and genetic nature of the emotions, the basic emotions we hear are *also* Beethoven's.

For this reason, anytime we hear a person perform music, that person, *as a person*, is exposed to us as well as the notes of the music. It is impossible for the *real* person to hide his true nature during performance. Anyone who does not want the world to see his innermost private identification as a person should never perform as a musician in public.

This fact about musicians is so obvious that it has been noticed and remarked upon for thousands of years. Here is a passage from Plato (427–347 BC) which gives the impression that he thought the character of the performer, here a singer-poet, was as important as the music itself. He demands a performer who is mature, who has accomplished some noble or illustrious deed and who is a good man!

> Let poets celebrate the victors,—not however every poet, but only one who in the first place is not less than fifty years of age; nor should he be one who, although he may have musical and poetical gifts, has never in his life done any noble or illustrious action; but those who are themselves good and also honorable in the state, creators of noble actions—let their poems be sung, even though they are not very musical. And let the judgment of them rest with the instructor of youth and the other guardians of the laws, who shall give them this privilege, and they alone shall be free to sing; but the rest of the world shall not have this liberty. Nor shall anyone dare to sing a song which has not been approved by the judgment of the guardians of the laws, not even if his strain be sweeter than the songs of Thamyras and Orpheus; but only such poems as have been judged sacred and dedicated to the Gods, and such as are the works of good men.[1]

The famous philosopher and geographer, Strabo (63 BC–24 AD) makes the point we made above. In a carpenter (who deals with rational measurements), he says, the character of the person does not matter. But in the case of a poet, and the reader must remember that poetry was sung at this time, he says the work and the man are 'inseparable.' It is impossible, he says, to be a good singer unless you are a good person.

> Of course we do not speak of the excellence of a poet in the same sense as we speak of that of a carpenter or a blacksmith; for their excellence depends upon no inherent nobility and dignity, whereas the excellence of a poet is inseparably associated with the excellence of the man himself, and it is impossible for one to become a good poet unless he has previously become a good man.[2]

The early Church father, St. Basil (329–379) holds this same principle to be true even for the members of the congregation who sing hymns! He admits that the chief value of singing psalms is 'to calm and soften the wicked spirits which trouble souls.' Nevertheless, he maintains that a 'bad' person cannot sing the psalms with spiritual success.

> Not if someone utters the words of the psalm with his mouth, does that one sing to the Lord; but, all who send up the psalmody from a clean heart, and who are holy, maintaining righteousness toward God, these are able to sing to God, harmoniously guided by the spiritual rhythms. How many stand there, coming from fornication? How many from theft? How many concealing in their hearts deceit? How many lying? They think they are singing, although in truth they are not singing. For, the Scripture invites the saint to the singing of psalms. 'A bad tree cannot bear good fruit,' nor a bad heart utter words of life.[3]

---

[1] *Laws*, 829c.

[2] *The Geography of Strabo*, trans. H. L. Jones (Cambridge: Harvard University Press, 1960), I.2.5.

[3] St. Basil, 'Homily 14,' in *Exegetic Homilies*, trans. Sister Agnes Way (Washington, D.C.: The Catholic University of America Press), 217.

There was a special, and difficult, problem for the Church in connection with its own professional singers, a fact that one finds numerous references to in early literature. Craig Wright has documented continued problems with the singers of the cathedral at Cambrai during the Renaissance. Aside from insufficient musicianship, he found records of peculiar disciplinary problems—such as one tenor who came to the divine service attired as a woman.[4]

The fact that the character of the performing musician cannot be hidden from the observer is sometimes mentioned during the Renaissance in the form of the question, 'can an out of tune player play in tune?' An example of this can be found in a famous work by the Spaniard, Fernando de Rojas (1477–1541). In this passage, the love sick Calisto decides to sing a song of love.

> CALISTO: Sempronio!
> SEMPRONIO: Sir?
> CALISTO: Bring me my lute.
> SEMPRONIO: Here it is, sir.
> CALISTO (sings):
> > *Can any grief compare*
> > *With what I bear?*
> SEMPRONIO: The lute's out of tune.
> CALISTO: How can a man tune it who is himself out of tune? What sense of harmony can he have who is himself full of discords? A man whose will refuses to obey his reason, who has barbs in his breast, in whom peace and war, love and hate, injury, guilt, and suspicions battle together? Here, take the lute and sing me the saddest song you know.[5]

There is an interesting discussion of our subject by Vincenzo Galilei (1533–1591), father of the famous astronomer, Galileo. He mentions in passing the aesthetic principle often mentioned in early literature, that an architect is to be more admired than a mason, because he uses his brain rather than his hands. This ancient prejudice is with us still in the example of some famous universities who find places for composers, but do not accept on equal terms performers.

With regard to our topic, he is the first philosopher to bring the listener into the discussion. Galilei contends that the performer who is a good man can make the man who listens to him a better man. There is some clinical research which supports this contention. Clinical research has proven that, good performance or bad, the music we hear makes a permanent record in our brain.

Thus, for Galilei, character was a necessary element of the definition of the most esteemed musician. After a few observations on deficient performers, those with no imagination or poor technique, he says those most esteemed are those who teach us something, meaning affect our

---

[4] Craig Wright, 'Performance Practices at the Cathedral of Cambrai 1475–1550,' *The Musical Quarterly* 64, no. 3 (July 1978): 297, http://www.jstor.org/stable/741504

[5] Fernando de Rojas, *La Celestina*, trans. J. M. Cohen (New York: New York University Press, 1966), Act I.

character in the manner of the ancient Greeks. It follows, he says, that the character of the musician is an inseparable component. There is also the suggestion here that the teacher who places emphasis on entertaining his students follows a very old model.

> For those who teach us a virtue are much more to be esteemed, and the rarer and more excellent they are the more so, than those who merely delight us with their buffooneries; first because it is a greater and a higher thing to know what another does than to do what he does, and then because every purely sensual pleasure ends by satiating us and never makes us thirst for any knowledge. And I say that they are even more deserving when that knowledge of theirs is combined with the highest character, as these are the things chiefly to be desired in the perfect musician and in every follower of the arts, in order that with his learning and his character he may make those who frequent him and listen to him men of learning and good character. In addition I say that it is impossible to find a man who is truly a musician and is vicious, and that if a man has a vicious nature, it will be difficult, or rather impossible for him to be virtuous and to make others virtuous.[6]

There was a rare Renaissance philosopher, Girolamo Cardano (1501–1576), who has left a music treatise which has a rather darker view. Cardano's education began under his father, a lawyer in Milan, who taught him arithmetic, geometry[7] and astrology. Music lessons were made possible, secretly, through the aid of his mother. In later years he would remember this music teacher, Leo Oglonus, for his high moral standards.

Cardano studied medicine, and received his degree, but was refused permission to practice because the College of Physicians in Milan were under the suspicion that he was of illegitimate birth. He was able to gain appointment as a lecturer in mathematics for the Piatti Foundation, which was the turning point in his career. He attracted large audiences for his lectures and published his first two books on mathematics in 1539. With this boost to his self-confidence, Cardano began to fight back against the doctors of Milan. He published a book called *On the Bad Practices of Medicine* which was immediately popular with the public.

> The things which give most reputation to a physician nowadays are his manners, servants, carriage, clothes, smartness, and caginess, all displayed in a sort of artificial and insipid way; learning and experience seem to count for nothing.[8]

Public pressure caused the College of Physicians to relent and within a few years Cardano became one of the most famous physicians in Europe. Receiving offers from nobles everywhere for his services, Cardano traveled widely and was always received with the greatest acclaim.

All in all, this was a strange man and before continuing with his writings it might be well to let him describe himself.

---

6   Galilei, 'Dialogo della musica antica e della moderna,' in Oliver Strunk, *Source Readings in Music History* (New York: Norton, 1950, 320ff.

7   The father was consulted several times on geometry by Leonardo da Vinci.

8   Quoted in Oystein Ore, *Cardano The Gambling Scholar* (New York: Dover, 1953), 12.

> Nature has made me capable, pious, faithful, meditative, inventive, courageous, cunning, crafty, sarcastic, industrious, diligent, ingenious, impertinent, contemptuous of religion, grudging, envious, sad, treacherous, magician and sorcerer, miserable, hateful, lascivious, solitary, disagreeable, rude, divinator, changeable, irresolute, indecent, quarrelsome, and because of the conflicts between my nature and soul I am not understood even by those with whom I associate most frequently.[9]

As we have mentioned above, this curious man had a rather dim view of musicians and their character, as the following passage demonstrates,

> Music is also of worth because it is a pleasing pastime and is useful for discipline and as a cultural value of life. Also, since it affords pleasure without detriment it is beneficial to all and especially to children.
>
> Yet if one considers our presently complicated [contrapuntal] way of singing, which consists of many persons singing together and which cannot take place at one's own leisure, since there is a need for fellow singers and since so many of them have dissolute morals, we conclude that this practice is really of no use to anyone. You find hardly any musician in our time who does not abound in every kind of vice, and thus such a musician is the greatest impediment not only to a poor and busy man but to all men in general …
>
> But since this kind of music has subverted my own home, so to speak, I will present the facts in my own case. For not only did I sustain a heavy loss of money, but what is worse, I corrupted the morals of my own children. It is hard to assemble four or five person who can sing readily. Since we want this activity to take place frequently it occurs during leisure time. If we do it at home the singers will be maintained at great expense and they will corrupt the characters of our young boys and adolescents, for most of them are drunkards and gluttons, also wanton, fickle, impatient, coarse, indolent, and tainted with every kind of unlawful desire. The best of them are fools.[10]

The greatest French essay writer of the sixteenth century was unquestionably Michel Montaigne (1533–1592). After an education in law at Toulouse, he became in turn a soldier, courtier, traveler and mayor of Bordeaux.

During Montaigne's discussion of his objections to the fact that professors are learned but not wise, he observes that professors can recognize bad qualities in literature but not in themselves. Here he adds a suggestion that the quality of a musical performer can not be separated from his quality as a person.

> Dionysius used to laugh … at musicians whose flutes were harmonious but not their morals.[11]

---

[9] Ibid., 25ff.
[10] Quoted in Clement Miller, *Hieronymus Cardanus, Writings on Music* (American Institute of Musicology, 1973), 197ff.
[11] Michel de Montaigne, *Essays*, trans. M. A. Screech (London: Penguin, 1993), xxv, 156.

Interestingly enough, Montaigne exempts preachers, saying that while the personal sins of preachers were 'shaking the truth taught in our Church,' he suggests that 'we must consider the preaching and the preacher apart.' On the other hand, he wondered if writers should be in the same category as musicians, reflecting, 'I never read an author … without curiously inquiring what sort of man he was.'[12]

The great Spanish writer, Cervantes (1547–1616), felt about poets as others felt about musicians, maintaining, 'a chaste poet will produce chaste poems, for the pen speaks for the soul.'[13] The Spanish playwright Lope de Vega has the main character in his most famous play appear more out of tune than her instrument.

> DOROTEA. I go there, Celia? May God fail me if I ever …!
> CELIA. Don't go flailing about and swearing if you expect me to believe you. You've been torturing those poor pegs for an hour, not tuning the harp strings so much as your own unstrung thoughts.
> DOROTEA. I removed a few because they did not ring true on the flat notes.
> CELIA. Those must have been your thoughts of Don Fernando.
> DOROTEA. You're quite right, Celia, for the genius of music, as my master Enrique used to tell me, lies not in skilled fingers nor in a voice well trained, but in the soul itself—so the theory of music teaches.[14]

The German philosopher, Henry Agrippa (1486–1536), in his earlier *De occulta Philosophia* had discussed the impressive references to the character of the various modes by the ancients, but fifteen years later he finds that in his experience music has been degraded in practice by the character of the men who perform it.

> Although men confess that this art has much sweetness, yet the common opinion is, and everyone may see it by experience, that it is the exercise of base men, and of unprofitable and intemperate wit.... For this reason Music has ever been wandering here and there for price and pence and is the servant of bawdy which no grave, modest, honest or valiant man ever professed … But in very deed what is more unprofitable, more to be despised, and more to be eschewed, than these pipers, singers, and other sorts of musicians, which with so many and diverse voices of songs, surpassing the chirping of all birds, with a certain venomous sweetness, like the Mermaids, with voices, gestures, and lascivious sounds, do destroy and corrupt men's minds?
>
> ……
>
> And yet for this, these musicians do much boast, as though they were more able to move the emotions than Rhetoricians, that, so much misled by their madness, they affirm the Heavens themselves sing, yet with voices never heard by any man, except perhaps by means of their *Euouae*,[15] drunkenness or dreaming.[16]

---

[12] Ibid., II, xxxi, 811ff.

[13] Miguel de Cervantes, *The Trials of Persiles and Sigismunda*, trans. Celia Weller and Clark Colahan (Berkeley: University of California Press, 1989).

[14] Lope de Vega, *La Dorotea*, trans. Alan Trueblood and Edwin Honig (Cambridge: Harvard University Press, 1985),V, ix.

[15] A joyous shout during the drinking festivals of Bacchus.

[16] Henry Cornelius Agrippa, *De occulta Philosophia*, I, x. The best modern edition, which is highly recommended, is Donald Tyson, *Three Books of Occult Philosophy* (St. Paul: Llewellyn Publications, 1993).

Martin Luther, in a dinner conversation, makes a rather back-handed compliment about such performers. Because their character is so bad, he says, it makes the music, by contrast, look good.

> Music is a semi-discipline and taskmistress, which makes people milder and more gentle, more civil and more sensible. The wicked gut-scrapers and fiddlers serve the purpose of enabling us to see and hear what a fine and wholesome art music really is; for white is more clearly recognized when it is contrasted with black.[17]

In the English Baroque poetry of George Wither (1588–1667), the poet suggests that some musicians have manners which might be improved by changing their repertoire.

> Many musicians are more out of order than their instruments … They who are better tempered, are hereby [reminded] what music is most acceptable to God, and most profitable to themselves.[18]

And John Milton (1608–1674) once remarked, 'a good song is spoiled by a lewd singer.'[19]

As these centuries of philosophers have made clear, we should not be surprised to discover the character of the player in his music making. Because we see the innermost essence of the player when he performs, it is amazing to us that this opportunity has not become the focus of music education, helping the student to come to know himself on the experiential side of himself and to develop experience in his understanding of his own emotions. It should be the highest calling of music education. And if music educators elect not to do this, then who else will? We leave it to the student himself to stumble his way through his youth, learning about his emotional make up not from fine art, but from his peers.

And now a little trade secret!

Conductors become quite expert at reading the character of musicians, as they spend all their time on the podium looking at the players faces while they are playing. Even when guest conducting an unknown ensemble, within a short period of time the conductor knows more than he wants to know about the personalities before him. In fact, it can be quite distracting as this personal input can easily compete with the conductor's concentration on the score. This, in fact, is why Herbert von Karajan elected to conduct with his eyes closed.

This competition for the conductor's concentration on the score is also why most conductors refer, in rehearsal, to people by the part they play and not by their names. The conductor has studied a Beethoven score, let us say, and he has learned to associate the music in the score with the instrument names. He immediately thinks, 'oboe 2, please play louder,' but it is an extra thought process, since persons names are stored on a different side of the brain, to say

---

17 Quoted in Walter Buszin, 'Luther on Music,' *The Musical Quarterly* 32, no. 1 (January, 1946): 92, http://www.jstor.org/stable/739566.
18 Nr. 26–27, 'Halelviah,' Hymn XXXVIII.
19 'Animadversions,' in *The Works of John Milton*, ed. Frank Patterson (New York: Columbia University Press, 1931–1938), III, 176.

'Rupert Dillingham III, please play louder.' The player is not offended by being called 'oboe 2,' because he understands he is responsible for that specific part of the Beethoven score. It is the same on the football field, the special recognition aspects of which is also mostly of the right hemisphere of the brain. In the huddle the quarterback says, 'pass to the wide receiver.' No one would expect him to say, 'pass to Elmo Cruncher.'

The brain, as has been conclusively proven in clinical research, does not ordinarily employ both the right and left hemisphere simultaneously. It is one side or the other. Therefore, on behalf of conductors everywhere, we plea: if you want distinguished music, don't expect us to make much sense on a rational level in rehearsal. Forgive us our errors in sentence structure, vocabulary, names and data of all kinds. We represent another world.

Women Not Allowed

> *No other creature is less clean than woman:*
> *the pig, even when he is most wallowed in mud, is not as foul as they.*
>
> Boccaccio (1313–1375)

IT IS BECOMING KNOWN TO MORE AND MORE PEOPLE, in spite of the efforts of history books to ignore it, that there was a long period when women ruled[1] and all the gods were women. This period came to an end between 2,500–3,000 BC when northern Aryans began to move into the Near East. So, the males have now had five thousand years or so to try to learn how to achieve civilization. If the reader doubts their general success, we can only plead that they be given a little more time.

Of course with the beginning of male domination a certain prejudice toward women began to be present and has continued until the present day. This issue appears in our book because it has relevance to music. In another book we will recognize actual women performers of music in the ancient world.

It is difficult to discover much about the most ancient periods of prejudice toward women for by the time the modern languages of the Near East and Europe begin to appear references to women have, for the most part, been left out. We might begin with an anecdote from ancient Persia about Cyrus the Great (585–529 BC). According to the ancient historian, Athenaeus, some three hundred female slaves attended to his needs.[2] Presumably this tradition continued for two centuries, for several accounts mention that when the Greeks finally brought an end to the Persian Empire, with the defeat of Darius III in 330 BC, they carried away 329 concubine musicians from the court.

During the high point of ancient Greek culture, ca. fifth and fourth centuries BC, the Greeks believed music was a means of teaching bravery, courage and noble, manly ideals. However, as we approach the Christian Era there was an apparent change in the quality of their music for we begin to find writers who then said that music inculcates 'effeminacy.' This attitude must have been present earlier in some areas, for, in an anecdote which would be retold many time over future centuries, when Cyrus wanted to change a defeated people from warlike to harmless subjects, we read that his solution was to take away their arms and replace them with musical instruments. According to Herodotus, when Cyrus heard that the Lydians had revolted, he consulted with Croesus, who advised him,

---

1 Isolated areas of women rule can still be found. The *Los Angeles Times* (1995) carried an interesting article on a remote village of Juchitan, in the Isthmus of Tehuantepec in Mexico where women control everything and the men do little. The men are happy.

2 Athenaeus, *Deipnosophistae*, XII, 530.

> Pardon the Lydians, but lay upon them these edicts, that they may revolt no more nor be any danger to you: send them an injunction that they carry no more arms; bid them wear tunics under their cloaks and soft slippers on their feet; and give them orders that they themselves shall play the flute and the lyre and educate their children to be shopkeepers. Soon enough, my lord, you shall see them become women instead of men, so that they will be no further threat to you as rebels.[3]

From about the same time there must have been some strong prejudice toward women in Greece, for a fragment of a poem by Hermesianax (330 BC), an elegiac poet of the Alexandrian School, claims that the great ancient Greek playwright, Sophocles (496–406 BC), was rewarded by the gods with 'the fair Erigone,' even though he had been so critical of women in his plays.[4]

> Now of a prudent man I'd have my say;
> Against all women would his raillery go;
> He won the hate of all upon his way.

Plato (427–347 BC) argued for the use of strong and manly music in education. In one place, however, we find his concern that music might result in effeminacy, echoing the principle embedded in the anecdote about Cyrus. From this time on this word, 'effeminacy,' will be used always in a negative connotation and, of course, the reference to the feminine is in contrast to other, 'manly' music.

For Plato, his concern lay in the eventuality that students (male *and* female![5]) have *too much* music!

> When a man allows music to play upon him and to pour into his soul through the funnel of his ears those sweet and soft and melancholy melodies of which we were just now speaking, and his whole life is passed in warbling and the delights of song; in the first stage of the process the passion or spirit which is in him is tempered like iron, and made useful instead of brittle and useless. But if he carries on the softening and soothing process, in the next stage he begins to melt and waste his spirit, until he has wasted it away and cut out the sinews of his soul; and he becomes a feeble warrior.
>   Very true.
>   If the element of spirit is naturally weak in him the change is speedily accomplished, but if he have a good deal, then the power of music weakening the spirit renders him excitable;—on the least provocation he flames up at once, and is speedily extinguished; instead of having the spirit he grows irritable and passionate and peevish.[6]

Plato returns to this point in another place, where he adds that too much gymnastics is also undesirable.

> Did you never observe, I said, the effect on the mind itself of exclusive devotion to gymnastic, or the opposite effect of an exclusive devotion to music?

---

[3] *The History of Herodotus*, I.155. Plutarch, in 'The Apophthegms of Kings and Great Commanders,' told essentially the same story, but regarding Xerxes and the Babylonians, commanding they should practice 'singing and playing on the aulos.'

[4] 'Fragment XVIII,' in Henry H. Chamberlin, *Last Flowers* (Cambridge: Harvard University Press, 1937), 61.

[5] *Laws*, 804e and *Republic*, V, 452.

[6] *Republic*, 411b.

> In what way shown?, he said.
>
> The one producing a temper of hardness and ferocity, the other of softness and effeminacy, I replied.
>
> Yes, he said, I am quite aware that the mere athlete becomes too much of a savage, and that the mere musician is melted and softened beyond what is good for him.[7]

The end of the ancient period of Greece begins with the last century or so, BC, and is known as the Roman Period of Ancient Greece. The decline of music is mentioned by several writers, as here by Athenaeus, who again used the word, 'effeminacy.'

> It happened that in ancient times the Greeks were music lovers; but later, with the breakdown of order when practically all the ancient customs fell into decay, this devotion to principle ceased, and debased fashions in music came to light, wherein every one who practiced them substituted effeminacy for gentleness, and license and looseness for moderation. What is more, this fashion will doubtless be carried further if some one does not bring the music of our forebears once more to open practice.[8]

It is interesting that Plutarch also uses the same word, 'effeminate,' to describe the decay in theater music. Art music, he says, had become mere entertainment music.

> The ancients made use of music for its worth, as they did all other beneficial sciences. But our men of art, condemning its ancient majesty, instead of that manly, grave, heaven-born music, so acceptable to the Gods, have brought into the theaters a sort of effeminate musical tattling, mere sound without substance.[9]

Athenaeus finds only the Spartans have preserved the old values.

> Of all the Greeks the Spartans have most faithfully preserved the art of music, employing it most extensively, and many composers of lyrics have arisen among them. Even to this day they carefully retain the ancient songs, and are very well taught in them and strict in holding to them … For people [are] glad to turn from the soberness and austerity of life to the solace of music, because the art has the power to charm.[10]

It was also about this time, apparently, that similar changes were occurring in Egypt. According to Diodorus Siculus, the 'virtues' of the old traditions of education were no longer respected.

> Music was not, in those days, a part of normal education, since it was thought not only useless but morally injurious, in that it created effeminacy.[11]

---

[7] *Republic*, III, 410c.

[8] Athenaeus, *Deipnosophistae*, XIV, 633.

[9] 'Concerning Music.'

[10] Athenaeus, *Deipnosophistae*, XIV, 632.

[11] Quoted by Henry G. Farmer, 'The Music of Ancient Egypt,' *New Oxford History of Music* (London: Oxford University Press, 1966), 265.

While this decline was progressing in Greece and Egypt the young Roman Republic was experiencing a kind of renaissance in the use of music in all levels of Roman society. Here we read of a period where women enjoy respect and take part in the music making, a period, of course, which the Christians would bring to an end. The scholar, Alfred Sendrey, describes the Roman scene:

> In general, contemporary records indicate that the tendency to practice music prevailed, at least in public life, in gigantic proportions. Music teachers and music schools furnished dilettantes *en masse*; it belonged to the *bon ton* of every bourgeois family to give their daughters instruction in lyre playing. Rich people employed multitudes of slaves, who made music day and night, to the despair of their neighbors. At banquets there was no longer any conversation, since music drowned out every attempt at it. A veritable invasion of virtuosi of all kinds flooded the theaters and concert halls, bringing with them all their idiosyncrasies, vanities, and intrigues.[12]

The early Christian Church fathers specifically diminished the importance of women. The foundation for their view was in part based on the declarations of Paul, the founder of the Church, in 1 Corinthians 11:3ff where he clearly makes woman a lower rank than man. Second, early church fathers seized upon the example of Jesus, whose birth was said to be not of normal circumstances. As the third-century Church father, Lactantius, puts it,

> What need is there of the female sex, since God, who is almighty, is able to produce sons without the agency of the female?[13]

Given this background, the reader will perhaps not be too surprised to learn that it would be centuries before the Church began to officially revere Mary,[14] the mother of Jesus, and it has never acknowledged Mary Magdalene, whom many scholars believe was the wife of Jesus.

St. Augustine (354–371 AD) was the only one of the early Church fathers who admitted to a 'normal' youth. We mention this in passing only because it resulted in one of the most memorable prayers of the early Middle Ages, 'Give me chastity—but not yet!'

For reasons we have mentioned, one reads very little about women during the 'Dark Ages,' a period during which the Church controlled all literature. To the credit of the Church, it founded institutions to care for girls and women, but by the late twelfth century these institutions in northern France were becoming overcrowded. We have a document by the abbot Conrad of Marchtal in which he says he is not going to take any more women into

---

[12] Alfred Sendrey, *Music in the Social and Religious Life of Antiquity* (Rutherford: Fairleigh Dickinson University Press, 1974), 379.

[13] Lactantius, 'The Divine Institutes,' in *The Works of Lactantius*, trans. William Fletcher (Edinburgh: T. & T. Clark, 1886), Book I, viii.

[14] The celebrated vow of celibacy was also late in coming and was instituted to solve a real estate problem, not a religious one. The Church had come to notice that every time a priest died, property left the Church and went to the family. The change in policy was quite successful. By the beginning of the French Revolution, the Church owned one third of the real estate in France.

his religious community. We quote it primarily, however, for the language he uses, which, coming from a Church official, reveals something about the Church's continuing hostility toward women.

> Recognizing that the wickedness of women is greater than all the other wickednesses of the world, and that there is no anger like that of women, and that the poison of asps and dragons is more curable and less dangerous to men than the familiarity of women, we have unanimously decreed for the safety of our souls, no less than of our bodies and goods, that we will on no account receive any more sisters to the increase of our perdition.

Because that language is so shocking, we would consider it an anomaly were it not for another account from about the same time in Germany. Albertus Magnus (b. 1193), Bishop of Ratisbon, decided to retell the story of the Sirens. The reader will recall this passage from Homer:

> When on another journey the Odysseus' ship passed the Sirens, he had the sailors stuff their ears with wax. He had himself tied to the mast for he wanted to hear their beautiful voices. The Sirens sang when they approached, their words even more enticing than the melody. They would give knowledge to every man who came to them, they said, ripe wisdom and a quickening of the spirit.[15]

When Albertus retells this ancient myth it is again his language which one finds so striking, language which betrays a deep lack of respect for women.

> SYRENAS (Sirens), popularized in poetic fable, are marine monsters whose upper body has the figure of a woman with long pendulous breasts with which it suckles its young; the face is horrible and it has a mane of long free-flowing hair; below they have eagle's claws, and above are aquiline wings, and behind a scaly tail used as a rudder to guide their swimming. Upon making an appearance, they hold out their young in full view, emit some sweet, alluring sounds by which they lull their hearers to sleep, and then tear the sleepers to pieces.[16]

This is the same period that one finds the troubadour tradition in France. Here is a large body of poetry composed by minstrels to please the lonely wives who are the victims of loveless political marriages. One is surprised to find that even here there were a few troubadours who seem to carry the old prejudice. One of these in particular, Marcabru, 'spoke badly of women and of love.' This troubadour, who had a reputation for 'malicious songs,' was eventually murdered by a lady who was the object of his music. Piere Vidal, another who was known for speaking badly of others, had his tongue cut out by a noble!

With the arrival of the early Renaissance, the spirit of the troubadours was clearly still present in fourteenth-century Italy. However, the case of Giovanni Boccaccio (1313–1375) represents some ambiguity. On one hand he left poetry which has many of the characteristics of that style. But on the other hand, there are many passages in his works, especially among his

---

[15] *Odyssey* XII, 39.

[16] *De Animalibus*, trans. James Scanlan (Binghamton, NY: Medieval & Renaissance Texts, 1987), 373.

later works, which treat women, generally, in a manner few troubadours would have understood. Judging by a passage in the introduction to his *The Corbaccio*, the origin of his problem with women may have been in his own experience as a disappointed lover. This passage certainly seems filled with self-pity.

> I happened, as I had often done before, to begin thinking very hard about the vicissitudes of carnal love; and pondering over many past occurrences and musing to myself about every word and deed, I concluded that through no fault of mine I had been cruelly ill-treated by her whom I had chosen in my madness as my special lady and whom I honored and revered above all others and loved far more than life itself. Since it seemed to me that I had received abuse and insult in this affair without deserving it, after many sighs and lamentations, driven by resentment, I began not merely to weep bitterly but to cry out loud. I suffered so much, first bemoaning my stupidity, then the insolent cruelty of that woman, that by adding one grief to another in my thoughts, I decided that Death must be far easier to bear than such a life.[17]

In a passage in his *Concerning Famous Women*, Boccaccio, sounding very much like a medieval Church father, argues at length on the dangers of Love, how it enters through the senses and how lovers fail to follow Reason. Boccaccio presents here almost a courtship manual for young gentlemen. He finds virtue only in the first stages of love, when it tends to improve a man's behavior—including the inspiration to study music.

> This must instill great fear in men who are solicitous of their well-being and must shake them out of their lethargy, when it is clear what a strong and powerful enemy threatens them. We must therefore be vigilant and arm our hearts with great strength, so that we are not overcome against our wishes. First a man must resist. He must curb his eyes so that they do not see vain things, close his ears like an asp, and tame lust with continual toil, because love seems alluring to men who are not wary, and at first sight it is pleasing. If it is well received, when it first enters it pleases a man with happy hopes, makes him adorn himself, encourages good behavior, *savoir-faire*, dances, songs, music, games, conviviality, and similar things. But after love through foolish consent has seized the entire man, conquered freedom, and chained and bound the mind and the fulfillment of desires is delayed beyond what had been hoped, it awakens sighs, forces the mind to make use of wiles without differentiating between vices and virtues as long as it achieves it desires, and it numbers among its enemies anything which is contrary to this … If the lovers do not attain their desires, then love, lacking reason and using his spurs and whip, increases their worries, heightens desire, and brings almost intolerable pain, which cannot be cured by any remedy except tears, laments, and at times death.[18]

In his *Corbaccio*, there are moments of real hostility toward women. In one place he argues that women were born to be slaves.[19] And then there is this unbelievable observation by Boccaccio:

---

[17] *The Corbaccio*, trans. Anthony Cassell (Urbana: University of Illinois Press, 1975), 2.

[18] 'Iole,' in *Concerning Famous Women*, trans. Guido Guarino (New Brunswick: Rutgers University Press, 1963), 46ff.

[19] *Corbaccio*, 25.

> No other creature is less clean than woman: the pig, even when he is most wallowed in mud, is not as foul as they. If perhaps someone would deny this, let him consider their childbearing.[20]

Finally, in his book, *Concerning Famous Women*, Boccaccio observes, 'these things cannot be accomplished without a great deal of talent, which in women is usually very scarce.'[21] Later in this same book he gives a rather clear description of his view of women's place in society, which includes avoiding singing!

> If a woman is to be considered completely chaste, it is necessary above all for her to curb her lustful and wandering eyes and confine them to the fringe of her dress. Her words must be not only respectable but brief, and she must speak only at the proper time. She must avoid idleness as a sure and deadly enemy of chastity, and she must abstain from feasting, for Venus is weak without food and wine. She must avoid singing and dancing as arrows of lasciviousness, and attend to temperance and sobriety. She must take care of her house, close her ears to shameful conversation, and avoid roaming from place to place. She must reject paint, superfluous perfumes, and ornaments. She must trample with all her strength on harmful thoughts and appetites, persist in sacred thoughts, and be vigilant. And, not to discuss the entire subject of real chastity, she must love only her husband with great affection and scorn others, unless it is to love them with brotherly love. She must not go without shame in her face and breast to her husband's embrace, even when it is for the sake of procreation.[22]

One can be sure that the Church was not coming to the defense of women against such prejudiced commentary. Indeed, at about this time, St. Bernardino of Siena (1380–1444) wrote a treatise on the subject of 'the proper time for beating a wife.' In this paper he cautions only against beating the wife when she is 'great with child.'

In spite of men like Boccaccio, the Renaissance clearly brought a gradual change in the perception of women. One who was sensitive to this problem was the famous French poet, Machaut, who placed great pride in his love songs. In his comments in the Prologue to his collected works, Machaut seems to be providing a lesson, even a sermon, to other men. In this work he has Love warn him,

> But above all else, take care that you are not emboldened
> To write anything full of disrespect,
> And never slander any of my ladies.
> Rather in every case you are to praise and exalt them.
> Know well that if you do otherwise,
> I will most cruelly take away your standing.
> Instead, do everything in honor and thus advance yourself.[23]

---

20   Ibid., 24.
21   'Irene,' in *Concerning Famous Women*, 131.
22   'Sulpicia,' in Ibid., 147.
23   Prologue, III, 21.

It is in the context of this important topic that Machaut, in another work, 'The Judgment of the King of Navarre,' has himself placed on 'trial' for having written unkindly about women. Convicted, he is given the following sentence,

> You must—the thing is certain—
> Compose a lay for the first,
> And agreeably, without resisting;
> For the second, a song
> Of three stanzas and a refrain
> —Listen how I qualify this—
> A song which begins with the refrain
> Just like the ones sung at a dance;
> And for the third, a ballade.
> Now don't act like you're sick about this,
> But respond happily,
> As we have commanded.[24]

Among the early Renaissance poets in England, there were some who had not yet grasped the changing attitudes. John Gower's (1330–1408) writings retain the medieval Church's negative characterization of women:

> Neither learning nor understanding, neither constancy nor virtue such as men have flourishes in woman.[25]

Even the more gifted Chaucer, following centuries of Church dogma, warns about keeping the emotions under control. In 'The Merchant's Tale,' he advises that, in order not to hinder one's salvation, even the lust of one's wife must be controlled by reason. Not pleasing her *too* amorously, he promises, keeps one from other sins.

> In mariage, ne nevere mo shal bee,
> That yow shal lette of youre savacion,
> So that ye use, as skile is and reson,
> The lustes of youre wyf attemprely,
> And that ye plese hire nat to amorously,
> And that ye kepe yow eek from oother synne.[26]

Such traces of old Church dogma can also be found in Germany, as in this example from Sebastian Brant:

---

[24] 'The Judgment of the King of Navarre,' trans. James Wimsatt and William Kibler (Athens: The University of Georgia Press, 1988), lines 4181ff.

[25] John Gower, *The Voice of One Crying*, in *The Major Latin Works of John Gower*, trans. Eric Stockton (Seattle: University of Washington Press, 1962), IV, xiii.

[26] 'The Merchant's Tale,' 1676.

> For lovers act like children too.
> They seldom speak a serious word,
> Their speech like children's is absurd ...
>
> Deprived are they of sense and wit,
> They dance about like fools insane ...
>
> Who sees too much of woman's charms
> His morals and his conscience harms;
> He cannot worship God aright
> Who finds in women great delight.[27]

Because of the Church's great local influence, Italy was slow to change its attitudes about women during the Renaissance. Some conservative philosophers, of course, were closely tied to the Church. A case in point was one of the voices of the Counter-Reformation, Giordano Bruno. Born in Nola, near Naples, in 1548, he entered the Order of Dominic at age fifteen, became a priest at age twenty-four and traveled in university circles in a number of countries, including England and Germany.

The Church was still attempting to deal with the aftermath of the rediscovery of the books it had attempted to destroy during the early years of Christianity, namely the works of the ancient Greek philosophers. Bruno was one of those leading the Church's charge against the old 'pagans.' He accused Aristotle of 'impurities, blots, with certain empty conclusions and theories' and 'uncultured ... offensive and pretentious.' All philosophers, monks and courtiers, he wrote, appear a fool to someone else. And, of course, he did not forget women.

> Women are a chaos of irrationality, a wood [*hyle*] of wickedness, a forest of ribaldry, a mass of uncleanliness, an aptitude for every perdition ...
> [Quoting Secundus], Woman is an obstacle to quiet, a continual damage, a daily war, a life-prison, a storm in the house, the shipwreck of man.[28]

Baldassare Castiglione (1478–1529), as a diplomat for the Duke of Urbino and Popes Leo X and Clement VII, had the opportunity to observe Italian culture at its highest level. From this experience came one of the most famous books of the Renaissance, *Il Cortigiano* (The Courtier), which is a virtual book of etiquette for the young gentleman. In this book he gives a rather old-fashioned sounding warning about the dark side of love. He has the character Gaspare[29] contend that women find enjoyment in causing this pain, observing that not only can women 'make men miserable as well as happy, and they can give them life or death as they please.'

---

[27] Sebastian Brant, *The Ship of Fools*, trans. Edwin Zeydel (New York: Columbia University Press, 1944), 13.
[28] Giordano Bruno, *Cause, Principle and Unity*, trans. Jack Lindsay (New York: International Publishers, 1962), 118, 120.
[29] Pallavicino Gaspare (1486–1511) was one of the younger members of this cast of characters. A Lombard, he died young after a life of illness.

> So they feed on this kind of satisfaction, for which they are so greedy that in order not to go without it they neither give their lovers what they want nor make them utterly despair. Rather, in order to keep them in a continual state of anxiety and desire, they adopt a certain haughty and disdainful attitude, and mingle threats with promises, and they like their slightest word or look or gesture to be received with rapture.[30]

On the other hand, one does find some hallmarks of the changing views toward women. In a passage where he discusses the inferiority of women,[31] he does acknowledge that in earlier times there had been women who were 'very talented in music, painting and sculpture.'[32]

Castiglione in numerous places treats the gentlewoman as distinctly disadvantaged as compared to the gentleman.[33] From this it followed that she should not engage in the activities of the gentleman, such as playing tennis for example. Of particular interest here are the limits he places on women in the performance of music.

> For example, when she is dancing I should not wish to see her use movements that are too forceful and energetic, nor, when she is singing or playing a musical instrument, to use those abrupt and frequent *diminuendos* that are ingenious but not beautiful. And I suggest that she should choose instruments suited to her purpose. Imagine what an ungainly sight it would be to have a woman playing drums, fifes, trumpets or other instruments of that sort; and this is simply because their stridency buries and destroys the sweet gentleness which embellished everything a woman does.[34]

There are other Italians of this period who continue the traditional hostility toward women. Giovanni Bardi (b. 1534) offered women as a kind of negative role model for the perfect musician.

> Just as among Moors and Spanish women one may see shameless and wanton customs represented in music and dancing, so the virtuous and perfect musician can represent the contrary, that is, songs and dances filled with majesty and continence.[35]

And there is this gloomy view of love by the poet, Pietro Aretino (1492–1556), in a letter to Ambrogio degli Eusebii.

> I warned you to resist the first assaults of love. It is a frenzy that begins by making you satisfy your lustful desires and ends with your repenting the pleasures you had.

---

[30] *The Courtier*, II, 145ff., trans. George Bull (New York: Penguin Books, 1967), III, 274.

[31] Ibid., II, 201.

[32] Ibid., III, 240.

[33] Another interesting observation is made by the character, Giuliano de Medici, that 'there can be no doubt that being weaker in body women are abler in mind and more capable of speculative thought than men.' [Ibid., III, 218] Somewhat more patronizing is Castiglione's observation, 'think of the noble poems we would not have if the poets thought little of women.' [Ibid., III, 256]

[34] Ibid., III, 215.

[35] Giovanni de' Bardi, 'Discourse on Ancient Music and Good Singing,' in Oliver Strunk, *Source Readings in Music History* (New York: Norton, 1950), 298.

When this same correspondent was thinking of marriage, Aretino became much more concerned.

> Leave the heavy burden of a wife to those who have the shoulders of an Atlas. Leave her nagging to the ears of tradesmen. Leave her notions to someone who knows how to beat her or can put up with them … And if you must have a son and heir, beget him on some other man's wife …
>
> But when the day comes when continence has mastered all your lusts, then I will really praise your sense and urge you to take comfort in Poetry.[36]

Gianfrancesco Pico della Mirandola (1470–1533), who was murdered by his nephew, Galeotto, was one of several important philosophers who, as a response to the Reformation, attempted to reconcile the ideas of the humanists with the Church. In one place, however, he returns to the ancient negative objection to music because it weakens man and makes him effeminate. He points, by way of evidence, to the failure of Orpheus to rescue Euridice, 'because he had been made soft and weak by his own music.' Pico then leaves us with an enigma, with no further explanation.

> I want to leave the reader this knot to untie: the same serpent which deprived Orpheus of Euridice taught him (that is, Orpheus) music, and prevented him from recovering his beloved Euridice through his own death. I do not want to disclose this secret any further. 'Let him who has ears for hearing, listen.'[37]

The greatest French essay writer of the sixteenth century was unquestionably Michel Montaigne (1533–1592). He shared the demeaning view of women which had long been voiced by the Church, as well as the Church's view of sex in marriage as a necessary evil. Consequently his view of Love places it below the noble love of true friendship among men. Love of women meant primarily passion, 'rash, fickle, fluctuating and variable; it is a feverish fire, subject to attacks and relapses … A mad craving for something which escapes us.'[38]

Montaigne found many reasons to doubt the institution of marriage. In one place he objects in particular that women failed to perform 'their matrimonial obligations' and that wives only prove their love after their husbands have died.[39] Marriage is a bargain, fettered and constrained. Missing in marriage is friendship, because,

---

[36] *The Letters of Pietro Aretino* (New Haven: Shoe String Press [Archon Books], 1967), 59.
[37] Ibid., 149.
[38] Michel de Montaigne, *Essays*, trans. M. A. Screech (London: Penguin, 1993), I, xxviii, 208ff.
[39] Ibid., II, xxxv, 842ff.

> women are in truth not normally capable of responding to such familiarity and mutual confidence as sustain that holy bond of friendship, nor do their souls seem firm enough to withstand the clasp of a knot so lasting and so tightly drawn.[40]

In another reflection of his prejudice, he seems to understand that women are becoming more sensitive about their treatment. Here, as a prose writer and not a poet, he says, 'OK, if they have to read, let them read poetry!'

> Should it nevertheless irk them to lag behind us in anything whatsoever, should they want a share in our books out of curiosity: then poetry is a pastime rightly suited to their needs: it is a frivolous, subtle art, all disguise and chatter and pleasure and show, like they are.[41]

Finally, the reader will recall, above, Plato's worry that *too much* music in education was harmful because it promotes effeminacy. There is a similar passage in Montaigne, where, although he only mentions 'the arts,' and not music by name, and does not use the word, 'effeminacy,' but rather 'womanish,' the reader will recognize the hallmarks of this argument.

> Both in that martial government and in all others like it examples show that studying the arts and sciences makes hearts soft and womanish rather than teaching them to be firm and ready for war. The strongest State to make an appearance in our time is that of the Turks; and the Turkish peoples are equally taught to respect arms and to despise learning. I find that Rome was more valiant in the days before she became learned … When the Goths sacked Greece, what saved their libraries from being burned was the idea spread by one of the marauders that such goods should be left intact for their enemies: they had the property of deflecting them from military exercises while making them spend time on occupations which were sedentary and idle.
>
> When our own King Charles V found himself master of the kingdom of Naples and of a large part of Tuscany without even drawing his sword, he attributed such unhoped for ease of conquest to the fact that the Italian princes and nobility spent more time becoming clever and learned than vigorous and soldierly.[42]

We can also document the change in the fortunes of women by a comment by Desiderius Erasmus (1469–1536) was the greatest humanist, scholar and writer of prose of the Low Countries in the sixteenth century. In a letter of 1521 Erasmus makes the interesting observation that he has discovered a man who,

> takes pains to give his whole household an education in good literature, setting thereby a new precedent which, if I mistake not, will soon be widely followed, so happy is the outcome.[43]

---

[40] Ibid., I, xxviii, 209ff. On the other hand, his essay, 'On Some Lines of Virgil,' which documents his wide knowledge of ancient texts on sex, is a brilliant argument for the equality of male and female in sexual practices. He concludes the discussion by observing,

> I say that male and female are cast in the same mold: save for education and custom the difference between them is not great.

[41] Ibid., III, iii, 927.

[42] Ibid., I, xxv, 162.

[43] Letter to Guillaume Bude [1521], in *The Collected Works of Erasmus* (Toronto: University of Toronto Press, 1992), VIII, 296.

What he means by 'whole household' here is that the man is now also educating his daughters! Until now, Erasmus admits that he was not entirely free of the opinion held by others that 'for the female sex, education had nothing to offer in the way of either virtue or reputation.' He attributes his change of opinion to the influence of Sir Thomas More and he adds that he doesn't think husbands should worry that educated wives would be less obedient!

During the sixteenth century in England there are more interesting comments regarding the nature of women. Sir Philip Sidney (1554–1586)), scholar, poet, diplomat, courtier and soldier, was a key member of Queen Elizabeth's court, seems very frustrated when he observes that all the philosophy on the greater status of men is silenced by the mere sight of a 'fair woman.'

> But that the beauty of human person is beyond all other things, there is great likelihood of reason, since to them only is given the judgment to discern Beauty; and among reasonable wits, as it seems, that our sex hath the preeminence, so that in that preeminence, Nature countervails all other liberalities, wherein she may be thought to have dealt more favorable toward men. How do men crown themselves with glory, for having either by force brought others to yield to their mind, or with long study, and premeditated orations, persuaded what they would have persuaded? And see, a fair woman shall not only command without authority, but persuade without speaking. She shall not need to procure attention, for her own eyes will chain their ears unto it. Men venture lives to conquer; she conquers lives without venturing.[44]

Robert Greene (1560–1592) also acknowledges this silent power of women, in *The Royal Exchange*, where he lists four things which 'do greatly dull the senses.'

1. Delight in women.
2. Cruel adversity.
3. Oppression through famine.
3. Too much prosperity.[45]

The old code word, 'effeminacy,' which was used in ancient times to suggest that music made a man more 'womanish,' appears again in late Renaissance England. We find it, for example, in a sixteenth-century treatise from England called *Toxophilus*,[46] by Roger Ascham, a tutor to the young Elizabeth I. In this dialog, Toxophilus has been explaining the many virtues of shooting, when Philologus introduces the subject of music by observing that it is a common recreation for scholars. Toxophilus then quotes the early physician, Galen, who contended that 'Much music marreth men's manners.' Toxophilus elaborates on this by way of expressing his own worries about the effect of music.

---

44 Sir Philip Sidney, *The Countesse of Pembrokes Arcadia*, in *The Prose Works of Sir Philip Sidney*, ed. Albert Feuillerat (Cambridge: Cambridge University Press, 1962), I, Book III, x. Sidney (1554–1586).

45 Robert Greene, *The Royal Exchange* [1590], in *The Life and Complete Works of Robert Greene*, ed. Alexander Grosart (New York: Russell & Russell, 1964), VII, 314.

46 *Toxophilus*, in *The Whole Works of Roger Ascham*, ed. Rev. Giles (London: John Russell Smith, 1864), II, 25ff. Ascham explains at length why shooting is the ideal exercise for the student—such things as tennis and bowling being too 'vehement.'

> Although some men will say that it is not so, but rather recreateth and maketh quick a man's mind; yet, methink, by reason it doth as honey doth to a man's stomach, which at the first receiveth it well, but afterward it maketh it unfit to abide any good strong nourishing meat, or else any wholesome sharp and quick drink. And even so in a manner these instruments make a man's wit so soft and smooth, so tender and queasy, that they be less able to brook strong and tough study. Wits be not sharpened, but rather dulled and made blunt, with such sweet softness, even as good edges be blunter which men whet upon soft chalk stones.

Toxophilus then quotes the old anecdote which maintains that Cyrus, after conquering the Lydians and desiring to keep them peaceful, arranged for,

> every one of them should have a harp or a lute, and learn to play and sing. Which thing if you do ... you shall see them quickly of men made women. And thus luting and singing take away a manly stomach, which should enter and pierce deep and hard study.

Toxophilus concludes by questioning whether Plato and Aristotle knew what they were talking about.

> Therefore either Aristotle and Plato know not what was good and evil for learning and virtue, and the example of wise histories be vainly set before us, or else the minstrelsy of lutes, pipes, harps, and all other that standeth by such nice, fine, minikin fingering (such as the most part of scholars whom I know use, if they use any), is far more fit, for the womanishness of it, to dwell in the Court among ladies, than for any great thing in it, which should help good and sad study, to abide in the University among scholars.

The actual word itself, 'effeminancy,' we find in Lodowick Bryskett's (1546–1612), *A Discourse of Civill Life*.[47] He begins by reviewing the Greeks' use of music in education, in which Bryskett incorrectly understands that the main point was that the education of music and gymnastics were inseparable. Next he manufactures a quotation by Aristotle to the effect that the study of music alone would produce a 'soft minded and effeminate' man.

Now Bryskett turns his attention to sixteenth-century music. He says that while many examples of corruption in his time could be pointed to,

> one of the principal ones, in the judgment of wise men, may well be the quality of that corrupted music which is most used today; carrying with it nothing but a sensual delight to the ear, without working any good to the mind at all. Nay, would God that it did not greatly hurt and corrupt the mind. For as music well used is a great help to moderate the disorderly emotions of the mind: so being abused it expels all manly thoughts from the heart, and so 'effeminateth' men, that they are little better than women: and in women breeds such lascivious and wanton thoughts, that often them forget their honesty, without which they cannot be worthy of the name of women. Not that I would infer that music generally is not liked, or unfit for women also: but my meaning is of this wanton and lascivious kind of music, which is today most pleasing.[48]

---

[47] Lodowick Bryskett, *A Discourse of Civill Life*, ed. Thomas Wright (Northridge: San Fernando Valley State College, 1970), 107ff.

[48] Henry Morley, *Ideal Commonwealths* (Port Washington: Kennikat Press, 1968), 109ff.

Finally, one finds the negative code word again in the works of the famous sixteenth-century Spanish playwright, Lope de Vega, whose comments about musicians in general were often less than complimentary. In his *The Lady Simpleton*, Otavio includes poets and musicians in a category with 'effeminate fops, the madmen, the idle with smelly make-ups.'[49]

In the *Fuente Ovejuna* a group of musicians are brought in to sing a song during a wedding celebration. One character responds, 'Call that a song? You didn't strain yourselves!' and another asks 'You think you could compose a better one?'[50]

Perhaps Lope de Vega was accustomed to hearing such musicians apologize for their performances, for he has Dorotea, in *La Dorotea*, comment before playing on a harp, 'The one thing about being a musician I shall not do is ask indulgence for all my deficiencies.'[51]

It is interesting to note that beginning with the Baroque Period one no longer finds strong negative comments about women. Perhaps it was because the Baroque itself, in music, was obsessed with the emotions, a subject which had to include women as well as men. Or perhaps it was because at this time the first women were allowed on the stage, where they had for centuries been forbidden. The leaders on stage included the first famous female opera singers and their fame must have given a certain legitimacy to all women.

It is one of these first 'prima donnas,' a soprano known as 'La Maupin,' with whom we will conclude this discussion. We are attracted to her for her amazing spirit, an outgoing and confident personality that must be recognized as a harbinger of a new era for women.

She was a celebrated actress and singer in Paris when she married a young businessman. Soon after her marriage she began an affair with a fencing master, with whom she studied the art of the small and large sword. When her husband was offered an attractive position in Provence, La Maupin, not wishing to give up her life in Paris, moved in with the fencing master. The husband began legal action and the two lovers fled to Marseilles where they both found positions with the local opera.

Soon tiring of her lover, La Maupin developed a passion for, and seduced, a young woman. Alarmed friends of the young woman captured her and for her own safety hid her in a convent in Avignon. La Maupin, however, soon discovered her location and, disguising herself as a novice, gained admission to the convent. La Maupin set fire to the convent and in the confusion carried off her young female lover. The young women's friend rescued her once again, but by that time La Maupin had lost interest and returned to Paris, where she joined the Opera in 1695.

---

49   *La Dama Boba*, II, ix.

50   *Fuente Ovejuna*, [II], 151. The musicians, no doubt, felt they did not receive the credit they deserved. In *La Dorotea* [IV, iii], Lope de Vega quotes an anecdote regarding Michelangelo, who apparently felt that he did not receive the credit he deserved. Lope de Vega reports that Michelangelo, tired of being called inferior to the Greeks, broke a foot off a statue he had made and buried it in order that when it was found and praised he could prove that he had made it.

51   Lope de Vega, *La Dorotea*, trans. Alan Trueblood and Edwin Honig (Cambridge: Harvard University Press, 1985), II, v.

When a famous male singer, Dumesnil, managed to slight her, La Maupin dressed in male attire and waited for him after the opera one evening in the Place des Victoires. When Dumesnil appeared, she insisted he draw his sword and fight. When he refused, she gave him a sound beating and took his watch and snuffbox. The next day, Dumesnil boasted to his friends at the Opera that he had successfully defended himself when being attacked by three thieves. La Maupin, of course, humiliated him by immediately revealing that it was she alone who had beat him for his cowardice, producing his watch and snuffbox as evidence. In a similar circumstance, another singer who became the object of her wrath had to hide from her for three weeks in the Palais Royal before finally making a public request for her pardon.

On the evening of a great ball given by Monsieur, brother to Louis XIV, La Maupin appeared again dressed in a man's clothing. During the course of the ball she insulted a young lady, whereupon three of the lady's friends, supposing La Maupin to be a man, demanded that she follow them outside where they proposed to defend the young lady's honor. While La Maupin could have easily avoided the fight by revealing herself to be a woman, instead she drew her sword and killed all three men. She returned to the ball as if nothing had happened and explained the situation to Monsieur, who found the story amusing and pardoned her.

Some time later La Maupin turned up in Brussels, where she had become the mistress of the elector of Bavaria, who was in residence there. When he tired of her, he sent an emissary, with a large purse of money, to La Maupin with an order to leave Brussels. La Maupin threw the purse in the emissary's face, declaring this a gesture worthy of a scoundrel, and left for Paris.

In Paris she resumed her success on the stage, but in 1705 announced her retirement from the Opera, surprising her friends with her declaration of devotion to her husband and her intent to join him in Provence. There, in fact, she remained in pious retirement with her husband in Provence for the rest of her life.

She died at age thirty-four!

– PART 2 –

ON ETHICS AND PERFORMANCE

The Ancient Artist and the Public

A VERY ENLIGHTENING AND VALUABLE ANECDOTE is found in the history by Athenaeus (ca. 200 AD). His source was apparently Herodotus (ca. 440 BC) and it describes an instrumental contest in the context of some ancient Greek festival.

> In early times popularity with the masses was a sign of bad art; hence, when a certain flute player once received loud applause, Asopodorus of Phlius, who was himself still waiting in the wings, said, 'What's this? Something awful must have happened!'[1]

Athenaeus' report that in 'early times' popularity was considered bad is confirmed by several philosophers contemporary with this story. In a fragment by Heraclitus of Ephesus (535–475 BC), the philosopher is cautioning a musician not to make the response of the audience his aim.

> What discernment or intelligence do they possess? They place their trust in popular bards, and take the throng for their teacher, not realizing that the majority are bad, and only few are good.[2]

And Plutarch (46–122 AD) noticed in the works of the earliest important Greek playwright, Aeschylus (523–456 BC):

> And Aeschylus also makes it a point of wisdom not to be blown up with pride when a man is honored, nor to be moved or elevated with the acclamations of a multitude.[3]

The ancient Greek playwright Euripides (480–406 BC) looked with disfavor at 'idle music' and wondered why artists who have the potential for doing so much good ('to heal men's wounds by music's spell'), would waste their talents by being satisfied with being merely popular. Why, he wonders, is it necessary to have entertainment music at a banquet, when the banquet itself is sufficient entertainment?

> Wert thou to call the men of old time rude uncultured boors thou wouldst not err, seeing that they devised their hymns for festive occasions, for banquets, and to grace the board, a pleasure to catch the ear, shed o'er our life, but no man hath found a way to allay hated grief by music and the minstrel's varied strain, whence arise slaughters and fell strokes of fate to o'erthrow the homes of men. And yet these were surely a gain, to heal men's wounds by music's spell, but why tune they their idle song where rich banquets are spread? For of itself doth the rich banquet, set before them, afford to men delight.[4]

---

[1] Athenaeus, in *Deipnosophistae*, XIV 631.
[2] Fragment 104, quoted in T. M. Robinson, *Heraclitus* (Toronto: University of Toronto Press, 1987), 61–63.
[3] 'How a Young Man Ought to Hear Poems.'
[4] *Medea*, 179.

From such writers, and the ancient Greek philosophers who follow, the reader will see that the philosophers and playwrights identified with an educated class who looked with disfavor upon the masses who 'knew nothing.' The aesthetically highest music, which we would call art music, they called noble and manly music. The music of the masses was popular entertainment music, often called 'effeminate,' to reflect the perceived decay in the quality of the listener of such music. Both Plato and Aristotle attempted to lay down principles which distinguish between what is art and what is entertainment and one can say that these principles have continued to define the aesthetics of both music and the theater to the present day. To be an artist or an entertainer is an ethical choice every performer must make and it is his intent with respect to the audience which distinguishes one from the other. In this and the following essays we will follow the philosophical commentary regarding the ethical relationship of the artist toward his public.

We begin our look at Plato's (427–347 BC) view of the audience by quoting a charming fable. We do this primarily because the fable illustrates the close tie between art music and religion which one frequently finds in ancient literature. It is also nice to read here that there are spies who report to heaven on which of us is honoring classical music.

> SOCRATES. A lover of music like yourself ought surely to have heard the story of the grasshoppers, who are said to have been human beings in an age before the Muses. And when the Muses came and song appeared the grasshoppers were ravished with delight; and singing always, never thought of eating and drinking, until at last in their forgetfulness they died. And now they live again in the grasshoppers, who, as a special gift from the Muses, require no nourishment, but from the hour of their birth are always singing, and ever eating and drinking; and when they die they go and inform the Muses in heaven which of us honors one or other of the Muses. They win the love of Terpsichore for the dancers by their report of them; of Erato for the lovers, and of the other Muses for those who do them honor, according to the several ways of honoring them;—and to Calliope the eldest Muse and Urania who is next to her, they make a report of those who honor music of their kind, and spend their time in philosophy; for these are the Muses who are chiefly concerned with the heavens and with reasoning, divine as well as human, and they have the sweetest utterance.[5]

It is in the works of Plato that we find the first extensive discussion of the nature and role of the public. We begin with a passage in his *Republic*[6] where he now calls the upper, educated class 'philosophers,' who alone are those capable of understanding his (rational) concept of Absolute Beauty. The lower class now includes musicians, as they have by his time become primarily entertainers who cannot appreciate this rational definition of beauty. The reader may not have realized the extent of the concert activity in fifth century BC Greece, but it sounds busy indeed with 'to hear every chorus, and miss no performance either in town or country.' In this passage Socrates is the narrator and Glaucon begins:

---

5 *Phdaerus*, 259c. The reader is reminded that much of Plato is considered to be a record of the teaching of Socrates.

6 *Republic*, 476c.

> Musical amateurs, too, are a folk strangely out of place among philosophers, for they are the last persons in the world who would come to anything like a philosophical discussion if they could help it; while they run about at the Dionysiac festivals as if they had let out their ears for the season to hear every chorus, and miss no performance either in town or country. Now are we to maintain that all these and any who have similar tastes, as well as the professors of quite minor arts, are philosophers?
>
> Certainly not, I replied.

Now Plato names the lower class, the 'sight-loving, art-loving, practical class.' The point he makes here is that the lower class is capable of appreciating art only on a sensory level, but lack the knowledge to understand anything on a higher level. In effect, then, he is establishing the basis for separating art into two categories, art and entertainment.

> And this is the distinction which I draw between the sight-loving, art-loving, practical class which you have mentioned, and those of whom I am speaking, and who are alone worthy of the name of philosophers.
>
> How do you distinguish them? he said.
>
> The lovers of sounds and sights, I replied, are, as I conceive it, fond of fine tones and colors and forms and all the artificial products that are made out of them, but their mind is incapable of seeing or loving absolute beauty.
>
> The fact is plain, he replied.
>
> Few are they who are able to attain to this ideal beauty and contemplate it.
>
> Very true.

This idea now receives more elaboration and the definition here may well have been the basis of the division of music into 'speculative' (theory) and 'practical' (performance) which we find from the sixth century AD forward. The meaning of the final sentence here is again that the higher class has knowledge, but the masses can only appreciate.

> And he who, having a sense of beautiful things, has no sense of absolute beauty, or who, if another lead him to a knowledge of that beauty, is unable to follow—of such a one I ask, Is he awake or in a dream only? Reflect: is not the dreamer, sleeping or waking, one who likens dissimilar things, who puts the copy in the place of the real object?
>
> I should certainly say that such a one was dreaming.
>
> But he who, on the contrary, recognizes the existence of absolute beauty and is able to contemplate both the Idea and the objects which participate in it, neither putting the objects in the place of the Idea nor the Idea in the place of the objects—is he a dreamer, or is he awake?
>
> He is wide awake.
>
> And since he knows, it would be right to describe his state of mind as knowledge, and the state of mind of the other, who opines only, as opinion?
>
> Certainly.

In another book,[7] Plato adds some interesting information on the public as part of his general discussion of the decline of music. Here we learn that Plato was fully aware that the Greek traditions of music practice came from Egypt, not to mention his own study in that country.

---

7 *Laws*, 656dff.

He was acutely aware that this inherited tradition had experienced a loss of discipline over the centuries in Greece, turning from the noble old purposes to one of merely trying to please the crowd, resulting, he says, in licentiousness. The cause of this decline, he argues, was a new freedom which replaced the old strict government control. With this freedom came popular entertainment music and with it a corresponding decline in the manners of the audience. Now, he says, they go so far as to shout and hiss[8] at performers they do not like.

> AN ATHENIAN STRANGER. Let us speak of the laws about music,—that is to say, such music as then existed,—in order that we may trace the growth of the excess of freedom from the beginning. Now music was early divided among us into certain kinds and manners. One sort consisted of prayers to the Gods, which were called hymns; and there was another and opposite sort called lamentations, and another termed paeans, and another, celebrating (I believe) the birth of Dionysus, called *dithyrambs*. And they used the actual word 'laws' for another kind of song; and to this they added the term *citharoedic*. All these and others were duly distinguished, nor were the performers allowed to confuse one style of music with another. And the authority which determined and gave judgment, and punished the disobedient, was not expressed in a hiss, nor in the most unmusical shouts of the multitude, as in our days, nor in applause and clapping of hands. But the directors of public instruction insisted that the spectators should listen in silence to the end; and boys and their tutors, and the multitude in general, were kept quiet by a hint from a stick. Such was the good order which the multitude were willing to observe; they would never have dared to give judgment by noisy cries.

As Plato continues his history of the decline of music he laments that now the idea of Truth in music is forgotten. This has been replaced by an aesthetic value which says there is no such thing as good or bad music, only whether the audience is pleased.[9]

> And then, as time went on, the poets themselves introduced the reign of vulgar and lawless innovation. They were men of genius, but they had no perception of what is just and lawful in music; raging like bacchanals and possessed with inordinate delights—mingling lamentations with hymns, and paeans with dithyrambs; imitating the sounds of the flute on the lyre, and making one general confusion; ignorantly affirming that music has no truth, and, whether good or bad, can only be judged of rightly by the pleasure of the hearer. And by composing such licentious works, and adding to them words as licentious, they have inspired the multitude with lawlessness and boldness, and made them fancy that they can judge for themselves about melody and song.

Because of the two-class society in ancient Greece, the reader will understand that the educated class held a very dim view of democracy ('How can you let ignorant people elect the leaders?'). It is from this perspective that Plato concludes this passage by suggesting that the

---

[8] This is documented in an account of Euripides once giving encouragement to a younger playwright who had been hissed by the audience. Quoted in Sir Arthur Pickard-Cambridge, *The Dramatic Festivals of Athens* (Oxford: Clarendon Press, 1953), 266. In one of the fables by Aesop (620–560 BC), a lyre player is driven from the stage by stones. See Nr. 121, in *Aesop*, trans. Lloyd W. Daly (New York: Yoseloff, 1961).

[9] We were once instructed, in a most heated fashion, by University of Wisconsin professor, Ray Dvorak, that the only way to judge the value of a university band was if it had standing-room-only audiences!

freedom allowed in music promoted a kind of democracy in the arts. He objects to this, saying in the final sentence, 'why don't the insolent masses listen to those of us who know better, we who judge by Reason?'

> And in this way the [audiences of the] theaters from being silent have become vocal, as though they had understanding of good and bad in music and poetry; and instead of an aristocracy, an evil sort of theatrocracy has grown up. For if there had been a democracy in music alone, consisting of free men, no fatal harm would have been done; but in music there first arose the universal conceit of omniscience and general lawlessness;—freedom came following afterwards, and men, fancying that they knew what they did not know, had no longer any fear, and the absence of fear begets shamelessness. For what is this shamelessness, which is so evil a thing, but the insolent refusal to regard the opinion of the better by reason of an over-daring sort of liberty?

Plato correctly recognized that the artist makes a Faustian compromise when he decides to create or perform according to dictates of the masses. Once the artist starts down that path he will be forced to produce whatever the public wants. How, he wondered, can the artist 'allow himself to be dazzled by the foolish applause of the world, and heap up riches to his own infinite harm?'[10] When the artist is questioned why he would make this choice, the answers are 'utterly ludicrous.'

> And in what way does he who thinks that wisdom is the discernment of the tempers and tastes of the motley multitude, whether in painting or music, or, finally, in politics, differ from him whom I have been describing? For when a man consorts with the many, and exhibits to them his poem or other work of art or the service which he has done the State, making them his judges when he is not obliged, the so-called necessity of Diomede[11] will oblige him to produce whatever they praise. And yet the reasons are utterly ludicrous which they give in confirmation of their own notions about the honorable and good.[12]

Plato was no doubt aware that he had taken a very narrow position on the performance of music and the audience. As if to mitigate things somewhat, in another book he seems to attempt, through a very 'rational' intellectual argument, to offer the possibility that one *can*, if one is self-disciplined, enjoy popular music without it resulting in licentiousness.

> Anyone who pays the least attention to the subject will also perceive that in music there is the same reconciliation of opposites; and I suppose that this must have been the meaning of Heraclitus, although his words are not accurate; for he says the One is united by disunion, like the harmony[13] of the bow and the lyre. Now it is the height of absurdity to say that harmony is discord or it is composed of elements which are still in a state of discord. But what he probably meant was, that harmony is attained through the art of music by the reconciliation of differing notes of higher and

---

[10] *Republic*. IX, 591d.

[11] This seems to be a 'principle' made up by Plato, or at least there is no surviving such comment by Diomede.

[12] *Republic*, VI, 493d.

[13] The Greeks used the word 'harmony' in a larger sense, the whole rather than one of the parts; indeed, it is often used as we might use today the word 'music' itself. The term 'symphony' was sometimes used to express what we mean by 'harmony.'

> lower pitch which once disagreed; for if the higher and lower notes still disagreed, there could be no harmony,—clearly not. For harmony is a symphony, and symphony is a kind of agreement; but an agreement of disagreements while they disagree there cannot be; you cannot, I repeat, harmonize that which disagrees. In like manner rhythm is compounded of elements short and long, once differing and now in accord; which accordance, as in the former instance medicine, so in all these other cases music implants, making love and concord to grow up among them; and thus music, too, is a science of the phenomena of love in their application to harmony and rhythm. Again, in the constitution of a harmony as of a rhythm there is no difficulty in discerning love, and as yet there is no sign of its duality. But when you want to use them in actual life, either in the kind of composition to which the term 'lyrical' is applied or in the correct employment of melodies and meters already composed, which latter is called education, then indeed the difficulty begins, and the good artist is needed. Then the old tale has to be repeated of fair and heavenly love—the love that comes from Urania the fair and heavenly muse—and of the duty of gratifying the temperate,[14] and those who are as yet intemperate only that they may become temperate, and of preserving their love; and again, of the common love that comes from Polyhymnia, that must be used with circumspection in order that the pleasure be enjoyed, but may not generate licentiousness.[15]

By the time of Aristotle (384–322 BC) the professional musician had become primarily an entertainer. In the course of making the point that this kind of music is not acceptable in education, Aristotle also comments on the relationship between performer and public.

> Thus then we reject the professional instruments and also the professional mode of education in music (and by professional we mean that which is adopted in contests), for in this the performer practices the art, not for the sake of his own improvement, but in order to give pleasure, and that of a vulgar sort, to his hearers ... The result is that the performers are vulgarized, for the end at which they aim is bad. The vulgarity of the spectator tends to lower the character of the music and therefore of the performers.[16]

In another place Aristotle distains the poet-musicians who think first of the audience, 'merely following their public, writing as its wishes dictate.'[17]

Closely related to this, he admits that just the fascination with the stage action, the 'spectacle,' can arouse pity and fear, but that it is better if they are aroused by the structure and incidents of the play. As an analogy with music we might think of the impact of the performance as opposed to the impact of the music itself.[18]

Aristotle concludes that no art can be a high art if it is addressed to everyone.

---

[14] By temperance Plato means something like self-discipline.

[15] *Symposium*, 187b.

[16] *Poetics*, 1341b.9.

[17] Ibid., 1453a.34.

[18] Of course the performance can also detract from the aesthetic experience. In this regard, Aristotle complains about bad stage business, citing aulos players 'rolling about ... pulling at the chorus leader. But this censure may have to do with the interpreter; it is quite possible to overdo gesturing.'

> It may be argued that the less vulgar is the higher and the less vulgar is always that which addresses the better public, an art addressing any and every one is of a very vulgar order.[19]

One of the last of the ancient Greek philosophers was known as Aristides Quintilianus and lived sometime between the first and fourth century AD. His treatise, *De Musica*,[20] includes a passage reflecting art and the audience. Some people, he writes, should observe everything, but the upper class should be much more selective.

> Concerning the art of delivery the following must be said. Of the bodily movements in which delivery consists, those which imitate ideas, diction, melodies and rhythms of a reverent and male character, and which incite us to manliness, should be seen and copied by everyone. Those whose nature is the opposite may be watched and imitated by the common people—but not all of them, and not by everyone. At any rate, people of noble nature and sound character should refrain from imitating and watching them altogether.

From ancient Rome we have some extensive comments about oratory and the public by Cicero (106–43 BC). He was a man who paid little attention to music, but some of his comments about the orator are worthy of consideration by musicians, as in both cases they concern a performer before an audience. The most important question he raises is regarding the difference between Popularity and Universality. Popularity, as we have seen, was usually taken as a negative by the early philosophers. But universality, as in the example of Shakespeare in the theater or Beethoven in the concert hall, means an artist has produced so refined a Truth as to be understood by all men. That surely must be a high accomplishment. Now comes the paradox. As pointed out by Debussy, twenty-one centuries later, an artist is most complimented when he is complimented by the real experts in his field; however, '*fame* is a gift of the masses who know nothing.' It was of this paradox that Cicero concluded that only the masses are the proper judges, not the experts.

> This discussion about the reasons for esteeming an orator good or bad I much prefer should win the approval of you and of Brutus, but as for my oratory I should wish it rather to win the approval of the public. The truth is that the orator who is approved by the multitude must inevitably be approved by the expert ...
>
> Now there are three things in my opinion which the orator should effect: instruct his listener, give him pleasure, stir his emotions. By what virtues in the orator each one of these is effected, or from what faults the orator fails to attain the desired effect, or in trying even slips and falls, a master of the art will be able to judge. But whether or not the orator succeeds in conveying to his listeners the emotions which he wishes to convey, can only be judged by the assent of the multitude and the approbation of the people. For that reason, as to the question whether an orator is good or bad, there has never been disagreement between experts and the common people ...

---

[19] Ibid., 1461b.27.

[20] Aristides' discussion begins Book II. All our quotations are from the translation by Andrew Barker, *Greek Musical Writings* (Cambridge: Cambridge University Press, 1989), II, 457ff.

> When one hears a real orator he believes what is said, thinks it true, assents and approves; the orator's words win conviction. You, sir, critic and expert, what more do you ask? The listening throng is delighted, is carried along by his words, is in a sense bathed deep in delight. What have you here to cavil with? They feel now joy now sorrow, are moved now to laughter now to tears; they show approbation detestation, scorn aversion; they are drawn to pity to shame to regret; are stirred to anger, wonder, hope fear; and all these come to pass just as the hearers' minds are played upon by word and thought and action. Again, what need to wait for the verdict of some critic? It is plain that what the multitude approves must win the approval of experts ... There have been orators in great number with many varied styles of speaking, but was there ever among them all one who was adjudged preeminent by the verdict of the masses who did not likewise win the approval of the experts?[21]

In particular, Cicero identified emotion as the universal element which captures the appreciation of the large audience, something which he found to be similar in both music and oratory.

> For just as from the sound of the strings on the harp the skill with which they are struck is readily recognized, so what skill the orator has in playing on the minds of his audience is recognized by the emotion produced.[22]

But now Cicero makes three qualifications, the first of which has to do with programming for the public. Here Cicero takes the position of the ancient Greeks and in his *Tusculan Disputations* he makes it very clear that to actually program at the level of the masses is something which the artist does not do.

> It must be realized that neither is popular fame to be sought for itself, nor obscurity to be dreaded. 'I came to Athens,' said Democritus, 'and nobody there recognized me.' A steadfast and serious man, to glory in his lack of glory! Or can it be that while the aulos players and those who play the lyre use their own judgment, not that of the crowd, to tune their songs and melodies, the wise man, endowed with a far greater skill, searches out not what is most true, but what the crowd wants? Or is anything more foolish than to think that those whom as individuals one despises as mere hacks and hooligans amount to something when taken all together? He will despise our ambitions and frivolities and spurn the people's honors, even when offered without his seeking them. But we don't know how to despise them until we come to regret our error.[23]

The second qualification which Cicero makes has to do with tailoring the material to the specific public. Sometimes the material itself is too complex for the masses to appreciate. He quotes an anecdote in which Demosthenes was reading a long poem and in the midst of his reading all the audience walked out except for Plato. Demosthenes is reported to have said, 'I shall go on reading just the same; for me Plato alone is as good as a hundred thousand.' Quite right, says Cicero,

---

[21] Cicero, *Brutus*, xlix, 184ff.

[22] Ibid., liv, 199.

[23] Cicero, *Tusculan Disputations*, V, 104.

for a poem full of obscure allusions can from its nature only win the approbation of the few; an oration meant for a general public must aim to win the assent of the throng.[24]

The third qualification Cicero offers his readers has to do with the fact that an audience consisting of the masses may not understand what he is talking about. For this reason, he had apparently observed that a particularly smooth speaker could win the admiration of the audience even though the speech itself was devoid of content.

> Thus, for example, if the wind instrument when blown upon does not respond with sound, the musician knows that the instrument must be discarded, and so in like manner the popular ear is for the orator a kind of instrument; if it refuses to accept the breath blown into it, or if, as a horse [refuses to move] to the rein, the listener does not respond, there is no use of urging him. There is however this difference, that the crowd sometimes gives its approval to an orator who does not deserve it, but it approves without comparison. When it is pleased by a mediocre or even bad speaker it is content with him; it does not apprehend that there is something better; it approves what is offered, whatever its quality; for even a mediocre orator will hold its attention, if only he amounts to anything at all, since there is nothing that has so potent an effect upon human emotions as well-ordered and embellished speech.[25]

It was perhaps for these mediocre speakers that one heard 'hired' applause, a practice which, needless to say, Cicero objected to.

> Expressions of public opinion at Assemblies and at meetings are sometimes the voice of truth, but sometimes they are falsified and corrupt: at theatrical and gladiatorial shows it is said to be common for some feeble and scanty applause to be started by a hired and unprincipled claque, and yet, when that happens, it is easy to see how and by whom it is started and what the honest part of the audience does.[26]

Finally, Cicero appears to have wanted to make some distinction between popularity and ambition. Even if popularity is bad, ambition on the part of the orator should not be considered a bad trait.

> Ambition is a universal factor in life, and the nobler a man is, the more susceptible is he to the sweets of fame. We should not disclaim this human weakness, which indeed is patent to all; we should rather admit it unabashed. Why, upon the very books in which they bid us scorn ambition philosophers inscribe their names![27]

---

24   Cicero, *Brutus*, li, 191.
25   Ibid., li, 192.
26   Cicero, *Pro Sestio*, liv, 115.
27   Cicero, *Pro Archia Poeta*, x, 26.

The next important Roman poet was Horace (66–8 BC), one of the greatest philosophers of early Rome. His aim as a poet (the reader will recall that most poetry was sung at this time) was to write poetry in such a way that others would think it so easy that they too could write such works, only to find out they could not.

> My aim shall be poetry, so molded from the familiar that anybody may hope for the same success, may sweat much and yet toil in vain when attempting the same: such is the power of order and connection, such the beauty that may crown the commonplace.[28]

This will no doubt remind the reader of a famous remark by Mozart regarding the reception of his music by the public at large.

> These passages are written in such a way that the less learned cannot fail to be pleased, though without knowing why.[29]

But if this were his aim, in practice Horace seems to have found the public incapable of accuracy in the ability to judge quality in art. He seems especially sensitive to having to compete with the reputation of the poets of old.

> At times the public sees straight; sometimes they make mistakes. If they admire the ancient poets and cry them up so as to put nothing above them, nothing on their level, they are wrong.[30]

But then, he admits, it is natural that men should disagree.

> After all, men have not all the same tastes and likes. Lyric song is your delight, our neighbor here takes pleasure in iambics, the one yonder in Bion's satires, with their caustic wit.[31]

In general, Horace saw the public of his day as being interested only in entertainment. He probably felt the noisy public had little interest in his art.

> I loathe the mob impure and forbid its place.
> Let tongues be silent![32]

His frustration was that the general public was only interested in spectacle, which were complicated entertainment stage works. Horace was well aware of the decline of the theater arts since the time of the Greek lyric poets and how the writers of his day too often succumbed to the entertainment demands of the audience.

---

[28] Horace, *The Art of Poetry*, 471.
[29] Letter to his father, December 28, 1782.
[30] Horace, *Epistles*, II, 1, 63.
[31] Ibid., II, 2, 58.
[32] Horace, *Odes*, III, 1.

> Often even the bold poet is frightened and put to rout, when those who are stronger in number, but weaker in worth and rank, unlearned and stupid and ready to fight it out if the knights dispute with them, call in the middle of a play for a bear or for boxers: 'tis in such things the rabble delights. But nowadays all the pleasure even of the knights has passed from the ear to the vain delights of the wandering eye. For four hours or more the curtains are kept down, while troops of horse and files of foot [soldiers] sweep by: anon are dragged in kings, once fortune's favorites, their hands bound behind them: with hurry and scurry come chariots, carriages, wains, and ships; and borne in triumph are spoils of ivory, spoils of Corinthian bronze. Were Democritus still on earth, he would laugh; whether it were some hybrid monster—a panther crossed with a camel—or a white elephant, that drew the eyes of the crowd—he would gaze more intently on the audience than on the play itself, as giving him more by far worth looking at. But for the authors—he would suppose that they were telling their tale to a deaf ass. For what voices have ever prevailed to drown the din with which our theaters resound? One might think it was the roaring of the Gargarian forest or of the Tuscan Sea: amid such clamor is the entertainment viewed, the works of art, and the foreign finery, and when, overlaid with this, the actor steps upon the stage, [and the applause is instantly heard]. 'Has he yet said anything' Not a word. 'Then what [excites the audience] so?' 'Tis the woolen robe that view with the violet in its Tarentine dye. And lest, perchance, you may think that I begrudge praise when others are handling well what I decline to try myself, methinks that poet is able to walk a tight rope, who with airy nothings wrings my heart, inflames, soothes, fills it with vain alarms like a magician, and sets me down now at Thebes, now at Athens.[33]

So, with public demand like that, what is an artist to do? Suetonius relates an incident during the time of Caesar Augustus when an actor, frustrated when a spectator began to hiss,

> called the attention of the whole audience to him with an obscene movement of his middle finger.[34]

In addition to the above examples of bad behavior by members of the audience (something still to be found today) there was also the commotion caused by the paid claque, persons paid to shout 'Bravo!' and lead the applause. Pliny the Younger, a first century AD lawyer and orator, wrote of his frustration with this custom after two of his own employees were approached to accept money for such services.

> Yesterday two of my attendants ... were induced to add their applause for three *denarii* each. That is all it costs you to have your eloquence acclaimed. For this sum seats can be filled, any number of them, a huge crowd assembled, and endless cheering raised whenever the chorus-master gives the signal ... If you happen to be passing the court and want to know about the speakers, there is no need to come on to the bench or pay attention to the proceedings; it is easy to guess—the man who raised most cheers is the worst speaker.[35]

---

33 Horace, *Epistles*, II, 1, 183ff.
34 Suetonius, *The Twelve Caesars* (New York: Penguin, 1989), 81.
35 *The Letters of the Younger Pliny* (New York: Penguin, 1985), 73.

Pliny tells of one lawyer-orator who, after several interruptions by the listeners declined to continue, observing, 'Gentlemen, this means death to our profession.'[36] What he means is that once you give in to the demands of the public, there is no turning back. Horace, reflecting on those who make the choice to give in to the desires of the public, was reminded of a fable about a fox.

> If the people of Rome should ask me why I do not have the same judgments as they, why I do not follow or eschew what they love or hate, I should reply as once upon a time the prudent fox made answer to the sick lion: 'Because those footprints frighten me; they all lead toward your den, and none lead back!'[37]

One reason to follow the public's taste was, of course, for financial success. Horace disrespected the famous Roman playwright, Plautus, for writing with this goal.

> Yes, he is eager to drop a coin into his pocket and, that done, he cares not whether his play fall or stand square on its own feet.[38]

For the true poet, says Horace, money does not matter at all!

The taste of the public had fallen so low that poetry was now within the scope of everyone. Everyone, he moans, is now a poet!

> The fickle public has changed its taste and is fired throughout with a scribbling craze; sons and grave sires sup crowned with leaves and dictate their lines. I myself, who declare that I write no verses, prove to be more of a liar than the Parthians: before sunrise I wake, and call for pen, paper, and writing-case. A man who knows nothing of a ship fears to handle one; no one dares to give southernwood to the sick unless he has learnt its use; doctors undertake a doctor's work; carpenters handle carpenters' tools; but, skilled or unskilled, we scribble poetry, all alike.[39]

During the early years of the Christian Era there is little discussion about any of the arts because the Church was trying to discourage the new Christians from the adoration of art in general. One does find occasional comments by the early Church Fathers, such as the following by Clement of Alexandria, which seem to follow the line of the ancient Greek and Roman philosophers that the artist should not aim to please the audience.

> We must not aspire to please the multitude. For we do not practice what will please them, but what we know is remote from their disposition.[40]

---

[36] Ibid., 74.

[37] Horace, *Epistles*, I, 1, 70.

[38] Ibid., II, 1, 174.

[39] Horace, *Epistles*, II, 1, 117.

[40] Clement of Alexandria, 'The Miscellanies,' trans. William Wilson (Edinburgh: T. & T. Clark, 1884), I, 378.

The third-century Church Father, Lactantius makes some observations which probably reflect the views of most of his colleagues. While he presumes 'pleasure of the ears' has the capacity of leading one to vice, he seems to regard music as not terribly dangerous because what we hear in music does not remain with us. Compared to the words of poetry, music just disappears. His last line here also reminds the reader that there was as yet no notation for music.

> Pleasure of the ears is received from the sweetness of voices and melodies, which indeed is as productive of vice as that delight of the eyes of which we have spoken. For who would not deem him luxurious and worthless who should have scenic arts at his houses? But it makes no difference whether you practice luxury alone at home, or with the people in the theater. But we have already spoken of spectacles: there remains one thing which is to be overcome by us, that we be not captivated by those things which penetrate to the innermost perception. For all those things which are unconnected with words, that is, pleasant sounds of the air and of strings, may be easily disregarded, because they do not adhere to us, and cannot be written.[41]

It is also worthy of note that he acknowledges, in the above quotation, the power of music to 'penetrate to the innermost' part of us. He mentions this in another place, where he is discussing the tendency of the senses to lead man to vice. Here he was disturbed by the powerful impact of music on the listener.

> But he who is carried away by hearing, to say nothing respecting songs, which often so charm the inmost senses that they even disturb with madness a settled state of the mind.[42]

However, he concludes, if one must listen to music, it should be music which has two aesthetic characteristics, that which nourishes the soul and that which improves you as a person. The only type of music which does this, of course, is music which praises God.

> Let nothing be agreeable to the hearing but that which nourishes the soul and makes you a better man. And especially this sense ought not to be distorted to vice, since it is given to us for this purpose, that we might gain the knowledge of God. Therefore, if it be a pleasure to hear melodies and songs, let it be pleasant to sing and hear the praises of God. This is true pleasure, which is the attendant and companion of virtue.[43]

During the fourth century we come to the reign of the emperor Julian (360–363), a rare leader who was also a true philosopher. In the following passage he considers the difference between universality and popularity. He believed that while some members of the audience, who have superficial taste, will respond to the outward appearance of the performance, one can be assured that the majority of the audience, even if uneducated, will respond to the genuine musical values in the performance. He also suggests that there were recognized aesthetic

---

[41] Lactantius, 'The Divine Institutes,' in *The Works of Lactantius*, trans. William Fletcher (Edinburgh: T. & T. Clark, 1871), I, Book VI, xxi.
[42] Lactantius, 'Epitome of the Divine Institutes,' Ibid., II,lxii.
[43] Lactantius, 'The Divine Institutes.'

principles of music itself which were commonly understood by good musicians. In the end he holds out the possibility that an artist can have it both ways, that if his art is of such a level he can be true to his art and at the same time be appreciated by everyone (universality).

> If one were to judge the best of two musicians, and were to clothe him in the raiment suited to his art, and were then to bring him into a theater full of men, women, and children of all sorts, varying in temperament and age and habits besides, do you not suppose that the children and those of the men and women who had childish tastes would gaze at his dress and his lyre, and be marvelously smitten with his appearance, while the more ignorant of the men, and the whole crowd of women, except a very few, would judge his playing simply by the criterion of pleasure or the reverse; whereas a musical man who understood the rules of the art would not endure that the melodies should be wrongly mixed for the sake of giving pleasure, but would resent it if the player did not preserve the modes of the music and did not use the harmonies properly, and conformably to the laws of genuine and inspired music? But if he saw that he was faithful to the principles of his art and produced in the audience a pleasure that was not spurious but pure and uncontaminated, he would go home praising the musician, and filled with admiration because his performance in the theater was artistic and did the Muses no wrong. But such a man thinks that anyone who praises the purple raiment and the lyre is foolish and out of his mind.[44]

There is commentary from quite an early date which confirms that the writers were fully aware of the importance of the environment of a concert or a play and the resulting aesthetic end. The Church philosopher Cassidorus (490–585 AD) was one who bemoaned the decline in serious theater, but in a letter answering some complaint about the behavior of the audience at entertainment spectacles, he seemed much more tolerant.

> As to their complaints of rudeness against the mob, you must distinguish between deliberate insolence and the license of the theater. Who expects seriousness of character at the spectacles? It is not exactly a congregation of Catos that comes together at the circus. The place excuses some excesses.[45]

The English Church philosopher, known as the Venerable Bede (672–735), wrote of a popular tradition among nobles during banquets to pass a lyre around the table in order for each guest to sing in turn. Bede mentions this custom in reference to the poet-musician, Caedmon, whose serious approach to poetry prevented him from participating in an entertainment setting.

> Others after him attempted, in the English nation, to compose religious poems, but none could ever compare with him, for he did not learn the art of poetry from men, but from God; for which reason he never could compose any trivial or vain poem, but only those which relate to religion suited his religious tongue; for having lived in a secular habit till he was well advanced in years, he had never learned anything of versifying; for which reason being sometimes at entertainments, when it was agreed for the sake of mirth that all present should sing in their turns, when he saw the instrument come towards him, he rose from the table and returned home.[46]

---

44 *The Works of the Emperor Julian*, trans. Wilmer Wright (London: Heinemann, 1913), I, 299.

45 Letter to Speciosus, in *Variae*, trans. Thomas Hodgkin (London: Frowde, 1886), I, xxvii.

46 The Venerable Bede, *Ecclesiastical History of England*, trans. J. A. Giles (London: Bohn, 1849), XXIV.

There was one English scholar of the late Middle Ages, Roger Bacon (b. ca. 1214), who was an original thinker and distinguished philosopher. Bacon studied at Oxford and at the University of Paris, where he received a doctorate in theology and then joined the Franciscan Order in about 1247. Unlike the gentle patron of his Order, St. Francis, Bacon was very outspoken in his disrespect for the masses, the 'unenlightened throng,' the 'ignorant multitude,' whom he says can never rise to the perfection of wisdom. For this reason, he maintains, the wise have always been an elite segment of society, separated from the masses. He found this also true in religion ('as with Moses so with Christ the common throng does not ascend the mountain') and well as in the universities.

> We see that such is the case among the professors of philosophy as well as in the truth of our faith. For the wise have always been divided from the multitude, and they have veiled the secrets of wisdom not only from the world at large but also from the rank and file of those devoting themselves to philosophy.[47]

He cites a book by A. Gellius in which the author maintained that the great Greek philosophers had discussions among themselves at night, so as to 'avoid the multitude.'

> In this book he says that it is foolish to feed an ass lettuces when thistles suffice him. He is speaking of the multitude for whom rude, cheap, imperfect food of science is sufficient. Nor ought we to cast pearls before swine.

The artist, Bacon observes, is above all concerns of the masses.

> Seldom is the poet's heart set on gain: verses he loves; this is his one passion. Money losses, runaway slaves, fires—he laughs at all.[48]

Let us see if we can summarize the core beliefs of these ancient philosophers regarding the relationship between the musical performer and the public. Imagine an artist, a flautist, is making his first public appearance and is performing carefully selected repertoire to demonstrate his musicianship. He appears, he performs and he receives very generous applause from the audience. He is elated and pleased, for everyone likes to be appreciated. At home he reflects with satisfaction on his experience and on the enthusiasm of the audience. So he decides to change his next program and to play works the audience will *really* like. The moment he decides to program *for the audience* he has crossed a line and he will henceforth be more popular, but he will have lost his soul as an artist. Like the fable of Horace quoted above, where the fox represents the artist and the lion's den represents the public, the fox is concerned because the footprints all go toward the lion's den, but none lead back.

---

[47] This discussion is found in his 'Causes of Error' IV.
[48] Ibid., II, 1, 119.

Thus will it ever be for the artist who chooses pandering. But there is another route, an artist can seek so high and refined repertoire and performance that he achieves universality. In this case he achieves popularity but not at the expense of either his art or his soul.

Finally, the reader should consider the implied question, above, by Euripides (480–406 BC), How much entertainment do we need? In our modern age we have hundreds of TV channels, not to mention radio, CDs and DVDs; popular music performances of all kinds; cinema; sporting contests beyond number and endless forms of entertainment on computers. How much more entertainment does the public need?

This should be Question Number One for school music programs. With all this endless available entertainment before the public, does there yet remain a civic duty for the school to provide the public with still more entertainment?

The Renaissance Artist and the Public

> *To speak of the public is really to speak of a mad animal gorged with a thousand and one errors and confusions, devoid of taste, of pleasure, of stability.*[1]
>
> Francesco Guicciardini (1483–1540)

IN THIS ESSAY WE CONTINUE TO FOLLOW the philosophical views regarding the artist and his public. We begin this essay with Francesco Petrarch (1304–1374), the famous Italian scholar, poet and humanist. He and Dante were central figures in the early Italian Renaissance.

Petrarch made quite clear his opinion that it was a fundamental mistake for any artist to plan his work with the audience in mind.

> No way is more prone to error or leads more directly to the brink of disaster, than the steps of the multitude. Almost everything which the crowd praises deserves to be condemned.[2]

Petrarch wrote again on the mistake of writing for the public in a letter to his brother.

> It's idiocy to regulate our lives not according to intelligent reason but to suit popular fads ... To follow the fashions of the vulgar mob, whose manners we laugh at and whose lives and opinions we despise, is to be more idiotic than the mob.[3]

As for himself, Petrarch claimed, in a letter to Boccaccio, that he held himself apart from the public.

> But, far from desiring such popular recognition, I congratulate myself, on the contrary, that, along with Virgil and Homer, I am free from it, inasmuch as I fully realize how little the plaudits of the unschooled multitude weigh with scholars.[4]

In another letter, Petrarch reveals that he aims his work for only a very small segment of the public, 'How can I please all? I have always striven to please only the few.'[5] This he believed was necessary because in any case the 'public' is in fact made up of *individuals*.

---

1 Francesco Guicciardini, *Maxims and Reflections*, trans. Mario Domandi (New York: Harper Torchbooks, 1965), C, 140.
2 'Remedies for Fortune Fair and Foul,' trans. Conrad Rawski (Bloomington: Indiana University Press, 1991), I, xi, 32.
3 Letter to his brother, Gherardo, in *Letters from Petrarch*, trans. Morris Bishop (Bloomington: Indiana University Press, 1966), 92.
4 Letter to Boccaccio, quoted in James Robinson, *Petrarch, The First modern Scholar and Man of Letters* (New York: Putnam, 1914), 187.
5 Letter to 'Socrates,' in *Letters from Petrarch*, 18.

> The varieties of men are infinite; there is no more similitude of minds than of faces. As the palate of one man—let alone those of many men—does not always relish the same food, so one mind is not always to be fed on the same literary style. So the writer has a double task: to envisage the person he is writing to, and then the state of mind in which the recipient will read what he proposes to write.[6]

He mentions this again in a letter to Boccaccio.

> It is important to know for whom we are writing, and a difference in the character of one's listeners justifies a difference in style.[7]

In the case of those artists who do seek to please the broad public, Petrarch finds the main reason is money. Here he exempts the highest artist.

> If anyone says that craftsmen are not seeking fame but money, I would probably have to agree as far as the common sort is concerned. But I deny it regarding the very best craftsmen. There are many indications of this—the way they persist in their efforts, regardless of the time they spend and the material losses they suffer. They even spurn cash lest they impair their fame.[8]

He mentions this again in a letter.

> Money, certainly, does not appeal at least to noble minds as a worthy reward of study. It is for the mechanical trades to strive for lucre; the higher arts have a more generous end in view.[9]

This topic also appears in his letter to Boccaccio, but he is careful to exempt himself from financial concerns. It is particularly interesting here that he refers to a general decline in the arts during his lifetime.

> Not that I am deploring my own lot, or looking for personal gain; I am mourning the common fate of mankind, as I behold the reward of the nobler arts falling to the meaner.[10]

Nonetheless, Petrarch probably included himself in this line from one of his poems:

> 'Philosophy, you go poor and naked!' says the mob, bent on low gain.[11]

In one of his letters, Petrarch points to a problem with the general public being its level of education.

---

[6] Ibid., 20.
[7] Letter to Boccaccio, quoted in Robinson, *Petrarch, The First Modern Scholar*, 192.
[8] 'Remedies for Fortune Fair and Foul,' II, lxxxviii, 204.
[9] Letter to Tomasso da Messina, quoted in Robinson, *Petrarch, The First Modern Scholar*, 221.
[10] Letter to Boccaccio, quoted in Ibid., 180.
[11] 'La gola e 'l sonno et l'oziose piume,' in *Petrarch's Lyric Poems*, trans. Robert Durling (Cambridge: Harvard University Press, 1976), 42.

> Experience, the great teacher, is on my side, though the silly, unteachable mob is against me.[12]

Petrarch appears to have believed that it was a waste of time to even attempt to educate the 'unteachable mob.' This seems more or less implied in his definition of a good mind, 'If it serves liberal studies it is a precious instrument; if not, it is ponderous, perilous and laborious.'[13] In any case he writes in more detail on the futility of teaching the general public in his 'Remedies':

> SORROW: It was my lot to get an unteachable pupil.
> REASON: You are tilling barren soil! Unhitch your oxen—why torture yourself? Quit bothering him and yourself. There are so many needed and inevitable chores; it is sheer stupidity to look for useless ones!
> SORROW: I have a pupil who cannot be taught how to pursue the study of letters.
> REASON: If he can be taught to pursue virtue, urge him to do that: and you will have enriched him with the best of all the arts. But if he cannot do either, leave him alone, lest you try pouring into a leaky jug water, which will not stay in it, and exhaust yourself in continual weariness.[14]
>
> ……
>
> Teach those who can be taught, do not bother with those who cannot learn, and avoid tiring them as well as yourself. Art rarely overcomes nature.[15]
>
> ……
>
> SORROW: I have a weak body.
> REASON: Cherish your mind and exercise it in its arts, and do not doubt that they are superior and longer lasting than brute strength—and leave manual labor to the peasants, the sailors, and the workmen.[16]

Petrarch seemed to have little sympathy for the poor teacher whose duty it was to attempt the futile duty of public education. In this same passage he makes a strange and surprising negative reference to the value of the liberal arts.

> Let them teach who can do nothing better, whose qualities are laborious application, sluggishness of mind, muddiness of intellect, prosiness of imagination, chill of the blood, patience to bear the body's labors, contempt of glory, avidity for petty gains, indifference to boredom…. What is more, neither grammar nor any of the seven liberal arts is worth a noble spirit's attention throughout life. They are means, not ends.[17]

---

[12] Letter to Laelius, in Ibid., 159.
[13] 'Remedies,' I, vii, 23.
[14] Ibid., II, xli, 103.
[15] Ibid., I, lxxxi, 223.
[16] Ibid., II, ii, 18.
[17] Letter to Zanobi da Strada, in *Letters from Petrarch*, 108.

He even had limited respect for his own teacher, Convenevole da Prato. In describing him, Petrarch anticipates the phrase commonly heard today, 'Those who can, do; those who can't, teach!'

> I had from boyhood a schoolmaster who taught me my first letters, and later grammar and rhetoric. He was an excellent teacher of both subjects; at least in theory, for in practice he was like Horace's whetstone, which can sharpen steel but cannot cut.[18]

Petrarch reflected on the extent of his own early education in his little biographical essay addressed to posterity.

> I learned as much of grammar, logic, and rhetoric as my age permitted, or rather, as much as it is customary to teach in school: how little that is, dear reader, thou knowest.[19]

Petrarch was not alone among Italian writers in his lack of respect for the public. The poet and playwright Pietro Aretino (1492–1556) was often contemptuous of the public, whom he mentions would actually hiss a work in public,[20] calling them 'unnumbered hired hacks of ignorance'[21] and 'those who don't know anything.'[22] He apparently included the popes in the latter category, for in one letter he quotes the painter, Giovanni da Udine, saying of his grotesques painted for Leo and Clement, 'I did them to please fools.'[23]

Equally strong views were expressed by Francesco Guicciardini (1483–1540), friend of Machiavelli and one of the important political writers of the Renaissance in Italy.

> To speak of the public is really to speak of a mad animal gorged with a thousand and one errors and confusions, devoid of taste, of pleasure, of stability.[24]
>
> ……
>
> To speak of the public is to speak of a madman, a monster full of confusion and errors, whose vain opinions are as far from the truth as Spain, according to Ptolemy, is from India.[25]

Giordano Bruno (1548–1600), philosopher, priest and astronomer worried about the reception of his *The Expulsion of the Triumphant Beast*, recognizing that 'the number of fools and the perverse is incomparably larger than that of the wise and the just.'[26]

---

[18] Letter to Luca da Penna, in Ibid., 297.

[19] Quoted in Robinson, *Petrarch, The First Modern Scholar*, 66.

[20] Letter to Galeazzo Gonzaga, in Thomas Chubb, *The Letters of Pietro Aretino* (New Haven: Shoe String Press [Archon Books], 1967), 173.

[21] Letter to Giantonio da Foligno, in Ibid., 52.

[22] Letter to Danese, in Ibid., 214.

[23] Letter to Niccolo Franco, in Ibid., 70.

[24] Francesco Guicciardini, *Maxims and Reflections*, trans. Mario Domandi (New York: Harper Torchbooks, 1965), C, 140.

[25] Ibid., B, 123.

[26] Giordano Bruno, *The Expulsion of the Triumphant Beast*, trans. Arthur Imerti (New Brunswick: Rutgers University Press, 1964), Explanatory Epistle, 70.

And Torquato Tasso joins the distrust of the general public found among the leading sixteenth-century Italian writers, when he warns another writer 'to avoid contempt from lesser crowds.'[27]

Marco Vida was born in Cremona some time before the beginning of the sixteenth century, at which time his first poems appear. His poem on chess (*Scacchiae Ludus*) brought him to the attention of Leo X. After the death of Leo X, Vida remained in the papal court of Clement VII, who made him Bishop of Alba in 1532. Holding that office, Vida participated in the council of Trent and died in 1566.

His *De Arte Poetica*, published in 1527, contains lines suggesting that he believed that poetry is a noble art and, as such, the language must be above that of the vulgar, common man. Hence, he seems to conclude, poetry is not for everyone.

> When first to man the privilege was given
> To hold by verse an intercourse with Heaven,
> Unwilling that the immortal art should lie
> Cheap, and exposed to every vulgar eye,
> Great Jove, to drive away the groveling crowd,
> To narrow bounds confined the glorious road,
> Which more exalted spirits may pursue,
> And left it open to the sacred few.[28]

We also have some commentary on the public by two of the sixteenth-century men we associate with music criticism during the Italian Renaissance, Vincenzo Galilei and Gioseffo Zarlino. Galilei, father of the famous astronomer, warns about depending on the public, the 'foolish rabble.' His reference to Reason and not trusting the senses is representative of the official Church dogma.

> I exhort you not to allow yourself, as the proverb says, to be deceived by fame, as do many who do not know the truth but only care about the approval of the foolish rabble, nor should you wish to be so credulous as to allow some things to please the ear alone without accompanying it by reason, because any one of the senses is fallacious, as you know.[29]

Zarlino, a famous early theorist, also warns about the artist trying to please the public, 'the ignorant common people.' He appears here as being especially concerned about the importance assigned to artists with foreign sounding names. He stresses this because there are some people,

---

[27] Torquato Tasso, *Creation of the World*, trans. Joseph Tusiani (Binghamton: Center for Medieval & Early Renaissance Studies, 1982), VI, 1213.

[28] Vida, *The Art of Poetry*, trans. Pitt, in Albert Cook, *The Poetical Treatises of Horace, Vida, and Boileau* (Boston: Ginn, 1892), III, 355ff.

[29] Vincenzo Galilei, *Fronimo* [1584], trans. Carol MacClintock (Neuhasen-Stuttgart: Hanssler-Verlag, 1985), 72.

who, having neither judgment nor knowledge, follow that which pleases the ignorant common people and sometimes want to make judgment of someone's adequacy by virtue of his name, country, native land, those he serves, and his appearance. So if being excellent and outstanding in a profession consisted in one's name, country, native land, service, appearance, and other similar things, I am sure that not many years would pass before no ignorant man would be found ... But in truth the opposite is the case: those who are great and famous in a profession are rare in number, and for each one of them, thousands and thousands of obscure, ignorant, clumsy, and crazy men are born, as one can see from any discussion.[30]

In illustration of how the 'common opinion' can completely misjudge a composition, he provides an anecdote regarding a motet by Willaert which had been sung annually, under the name of Josquin, by the papal choir in Rome.

When Willaert came from Flanders to Rome at the time of Leo X and found himself at the place where this motet was being sung, he saw that it was ascribed to Josquin. When he said that it was his own, as it really was, so great was the malignity or (to put it more mildly) the ignorance of the singers, that they never wanted to sing it again.

There was one Italian writer who ignored the advice of the philosophers and had sufficient faith in the public to leave his book to their judgment. Baldassare Castiglione (1478–1529), as a diplomat for the Duke of Urbino and Popes Leo X and Clement VII, had the opportunity to observe Italian culture at its highest level. From this experience came one of the most famous books of the Renaissance, *Il Cortigiano* (*The Courtier*), which attempts to describe the attributes of the perfect gentleman and lady from the sixteenth-century perspective.

Castiglione himself trusted the ability of the general public to judge his book as literature, even if they judged on the basis of instinct and not knowledge. He probably felt that in the mass public he could depend on what we call today Universality, that quality in an art work or work of literature which speaks to all men. Therefore, he says, he leaves the defense of his book, against all accusations,

to the tribunal of public opinion, because more often than not, although the many may not understand everything, they can tell by natural instinct what seems good or bad, and, without being able to give any reason for it, they enjoy and love the one and reject and despise the other. Therefore if the book meets with general approval, I shall take it that it is good and believe that it will survive; and if, on the other hand, it fails to please, I shall take it that it is bad and shall at once accept that it must sink into obscurity.[31]

Beyond that, he reflects, Time, the father of truth and a dispassionate judge, will pronounce a sentence of life or death upon his book.

We suspect he came to this unusual trust in the uneducated public partly because he had come to believe that writing for individuals made no sense for individuals all have different views. This was most conspicuous to him in the example of Love.

---

30 Gioseffo Zarlino, *On the Modes*, trans. Vered Cohen (New Haven: Yale University Press, 1983), 107.

31 *The Courtier*, trans. George Bull (New York: Penguin Books, 1967), Prologue, 36.

Therefore it often happens that what one person finds adorable another finds most detestable.[32]

He attributes this inconsistency from man to man as the work of Nature, who being fond of variety 'has made one man sensible in regard to one thing and another in regard to something else.' This explains the variety of preferences among individuals.

> One man [is] foolish [for] verse, another in music, another in dancing, another in ballet, another in riding and another in fencing: each according to his own innermost vibrations.

The greatest French essay writer of the sixteenth century was unquestionably Michel Montaigne (1533–1592). He joins the majority of philosophers in his distrust of the public.

> Let us leave aside the ordinary people, they have no self-awareness; they never judge themselves and let most of their natural faculties stand idle.[33]

He was also distrustful of the views of the public because the public no longer represents individual views but took on a 'mob' character of its own. He observed, 'it is not enough to withdraw from the mob … we have to withdraw from such attributes of the mob as are within us.'[34] In another place he reflects on the danger to the artist when he is influenced by the public.

> Whether it is art or nature which stamps on us that characteristic of living by what others say, it does us much more harm than good. We cheat ourselves of what is rightly useful to us in order to conform our appearances to the common opinion. We are not so much concerned with what the actual nature of our being is within us, as with how it is perceived by the public.[35]

On the other hand, Montaigne wondered if the artist rejects the opinion of the public, does it follow that he creates only for himself? Perhaps, says Montaigne,

> Remember the man who was asked why he toiled so hard at an art which few could ever know about: 'For me a few are enough; one is enough; having none is enough.'[36]

This reminds us of the story of Michelangelo who, as his huge marble statues for the tomb of Julius II were being pushed against a wall of St. Peter's in Rome, suddenly asked the workers to stop. He ran behind one of the statues and began to polish a spot on the back side. The workers were astonished, saying, 'but that side will be against the wall for eternity and no one will ever see it!' Michalangelo responded quietly, 'I will.'

---

[32] Ibid., I, 46ff.

[33] Michel de Montaigne, *Essays*, trans. M. A. Screech (London: Penguin, 1993), II, xii, 559.

[34] Ibid., I, xxxix, 268ff.

[35] Ibid., III, ix, 1081.

[36] Ibid., I, xxxix, 277.

An anonymous Spanish author, who is quoted in the *Lazarillo de Tormes* (1554), disagrees, saying no artist creates for just one person.

> Few would write for a single reader, for writing is a hard job; and writers who have done their work wish to be rewarded, not with money, but with the knowledge that their works are widely known and read, and—if the merit it—praised. In this regard Cicero tells us: 'The desire to be held in esteem creates all the arts.'
> The same thing holds true for those who practice the Arts and Letters.[37]

The most enlightened of sixteenth-century Spanish philosophers was Juan Vives (1492–1540). His experience as a student at the University of Paris turned him against Scholasticism and his attacks on this old Church view of philosophy brought him to the attention of Erasmus and Henry VIII, who invited him to England. In his *Introduction to Wisdom*, an early treatise on education, Vives was particularly suspicious of anything 'a multitude approves with consensus.'

> There is nothing we ought more to strive for than to lift the student of wisdom above the emotions of the common crowd.[38]

Miguel de Cervantes (1547–1616) addresses a paradox which we associate with a comment made by Debussy. Debussy observed that while an artist is most complimented, and finds the most satisfaction, when he is complimented by the real experts in his field, nevertheless, '*fame* is a gift of the masses who know nothing.' In *Don Quijote*, Cervantes presents the same irony when he introduces a priest who had contemplated writing prose, but then changed his mind.

> I realized that there are many more fools than wise men; it's better to be praised by the smaller company of wise men than mocked by the larger crowd of idiots, nor do I have any interest in subjecting myself to the jumbled judgment of the haughty mob, which is exactly what most of the people who read such books are.[39]

And the same observation was shared by the great Spanish playwright, Lope de Vega (1562–1635). In his *Justice Without Revenge*, he writes,

> I admit that I should like to be famous among wise men, men of science and letters, for fame among the ignorant herd is not true fame, but a harvest where those who sow senseless acts reap worthless praise.[40]

---

[37] Anonymous, Lazarillo de Tormes, in Angel Flores, ed., *Masterpieces of he Spanish Golden Age* (New York: Holt, Reinhart, 1963), Prologue.

[38] Juan Vives, *Introduction ad Sapientiam*, in Marian Tobriner, ed., *Introduction to Wisdom* (New York: Teachers College Press, 1968), 99.

[39] Miguel de Cervantes, *Don Quijote*, trans. Burton Raffel (New York: Norton, 1995, I, xlviii.

[40] *Justice Without Revenge*, in *Lope de Vega, Five Plays*, trans. Jill Booty (New York: HIll and Wang, 1961), 239.

In general, de Vega had no respect for the views of the public. In the above play there is a passage which reads,

> The common herd is no judge of truth, and they are fools that base their good name on what crude minds believe. Common opinion is inconstant and variable, not ruled by Reason, but by the personal jealousies of those that will tell any lie to satisfy their thirst for news and gossip.[41]

In *Acting is Believing*, he again refers to the 'ignorant mob' and also gives a hint of the size of the sixteenth-century theater audiences.

> [Regarding a play with lots of stage machinery] But they usually amaze the ignorant mob and bring in more money than good plays, because they talk nonsense; and even if a couple of people take offense, there are still over five hundred who like it.[42]

In the end, Lope de Vega seems resigned to a predestined reaction by the general public:

> A friendly audience applauds and it is called a good play. Enemies will hiss and report it a bad play.

At the end of a very lengthy epic poem by the sixteenth-century Spanish poet, Luis de Camoes, a musician addresses his Muse complaining that he is exhausted and discouraged from singing to an audience which pays no attention.

> No more, my Muse, no more; my Harp's ill strung,
> Heavy, and out of tune, and my Voice hoarse:
> And, not with singing, but to see I've sung
> To a deaf people and without remorse.[43]

One of the philosophers who was most outspoken against the importance of the public was Desiderius Erasmus (1469–1536), the greatest humanist, scholar and writer of prose of the sixteenth century. He was born near Rotterdam and left an orphan while still a teenager. The executor of his parents' estate, in order obtain everything for himself, gave Erasmus over to a monastic career. Erasmus in time became an ordained priest and, although he studied at the University of Paris, his viewpoints always reflected to a surprising degree his background in Church dogma.

Throughout his writings Erasmus displays a pronounced contempt for the general public. His most frequent complaint has to do with the ability of the masses to judge, as he mentions in a letter to the archbishop of Canterbury:

> I cannot but wonder at the absurd judgment of the multitude.[44]

---

[41] Ibid., 233ff.
[42] Lope de Vega, *Lo fingido verdadero*, trans. Michael McGaha (San Antonio: Trinity University Press, 1986), 69.
[43] Luis de Camoes, *The Lusiads*, trans. Richard Fanshawe [1655], ed. Geoffrey Bullough (Carbondale: Southern Illinois University Press, 1963), X, cxlv.
[44] Letter to William Warham [1516], quoted in *The Collected Works of Erasmus* (Toronto: University of Toronto Press, 1992), III, 257.

A similar disdain for the public is expressed in a passage in which the main subject is the critic. He writes that he takes pity on the ancient actors who had to try to satisfy their audience,

> that motley throng, truly a beast of many heads, few of whose members have the same tastes, nor are they always consistent, and what is worse, the greater part of them are led by prejudice rather than judgment. On their thumbs [approval] the poor mountebank is wholly dependent; he must worship the lowest of the mob.[45]

He mentions this again in a warning he gives a young prince.

> The true prince should avoid the degrading opinions and interests of the common folk to the same extent that the common run of princes are keen to avoid the dress and life-style of the lower classes. The one thing which he should consider degrading, low, and unbecoming to him is to think like the common people, who are never pleased by the best things.[46]

And again in a letter,

> Don't you know that the more wholesome something is, the less it is popular and the less it gains ground?[47]

In fact, in one of the earliest poems of Erasmus, composed in 1489, he blames the judgment of the general public for the loss of ancient poetry.

> I am forced (but what a shame!) by a
> host of bumpkins more numerous even than the stars.
> This arrogant herd, always goaded by their
> fierce passions, tramples under their worthless
> feet (Oh what a crime!) poems dear to bygone ages.[48]

Thus we can understand that it was not his goal to please the multitude, as he explains in a poem on the title-page of his *Enchiridion* (1503).

> I do not care about the praise or the insults of
> the superficial mob. The fine thing is to please
> either the learned or the pious. If I happen to
> do either of these, it is more than I hoped for.[49]

---

45 Letter to Pedro Ruiz de la Mota [1522], in Ibid., IX, 60.
46 'The Education of a Christian Prince,' [1516] in Ibid., XXVII, 214.
47 Letter to George Spalatin [1516], in *Luther's Works* (St. Louis: Concordia, 1961), XLVIII, 35.
48 'A Defense ... against Barbarous Persons ...,' in Ibid., LXXXV, 183ff.
49 Quoted in Ibid., LXXXV, 75.

Heinrich Glarean (1488–1563) of Switzerland did his higher education at the University of Köln. Glarean was a man of many talents as is testified to in numerous letters by Erasmus, who gives the impression that he was unusually proficient in all the Liberal Arts. His *Dodecachordon* (1547) is a treatise which treats all elements of music theory in very great detail. Glarean, fully aware of this, reflects on the impression his work will have on the public.

> Perhaps we have treated this in more detail than is necessary But it had to be done for the state of mind of the masses, to whom nothing is explained sufficiently.[50]

In another place, however, he seems to suggest the difficulty lay with the professors as much as the minds of the masses.

> If by chance this has seemed insufficiently clear to anyone, I beg him to remember how uneducated and unpolished our present age is, that among the highly learned, even among those teaching mathematics, not one in twenty has a clear conception of this matter.[51]

The only sixteenth-century English poet we have found who devoted much attention to the ability of the general public to judge matters of art was Thomas More. In a poem called, 'On Fame and Popular Opinion,' he cautions, don't trust the public.

> Most men congratulate themselves if they attain to fame,
> Empty though it is; and, because they are light-minded,
> They are lifted to the stars by the fickle wind of opinion.
> Why do you derive satisfaction from the comments of the populace?
> In their blindness they often interpret what is best as a failing
> And thoughtlessly approve what is very reprehensible.
> You hang everlastingly upon a stranger's opinion
> For fear that some cobbler will retract the praise he has conferred.[52]

Thomas Nashe reminds us that this principle is expressed in the field of music in the apparent fact that the common man requires common music.

> So senseless, so wavering is the light unconstant multitude, that they will dance after every man's pipe.[53]

---

50 See Glarean, *Dodecachordon*, trans. Clement Miller (American Institute of Musicology, 1965), I, 79.
51 Ibid., I, 133. Glarean here was reviewing the history of the development of the cithara.
52 *The Complete Works of St. Thomas More* (New Haven: Yale University Press, 1984), III, Pt. 2, 175.
53 Thomas Nashe, in his *Pierce Penilesse His Supplication to the Devil* [1592], in *The Works of Thomas Nashe*, ed. Ronald McKerrow (Oxford: Blackwell, 1966), I, 225.

The Baroque Artist and the Public

THIS IS THE THIRD IN A SERIES OF FOUR ESSAYS which consider philosophical commentary on the performer and his public. During the ancient periods of Greece and Rome, the Middle Ages and the Renaissance the philosophers were mostly concerned with the fact that the masses were uneducated and uncultured.

With the arrival of the Baroque Period a significant change occurs in the development of Western music and it is called Italian Opera. Opera was born in Italy at the beginning of the seventeenth century with the intent to recreate what they imagined ancient Greek tragedy to be, a noble, serious stage work using music as a means of filling out the emotions of the story. Unfortunately, by the mid seventeenth century the character of opera had begun to change dramatically and it became instead an entertainment medium. Sharing much with today's daytime television (young lady in an impossible plot), it spread all over Europe as the latest entertainment craze. This, of course, changed the entire question of the artist and the public, as the new values created strong pressure on the artist to become an entertainer.

One can see this change to an entertainment emphasis was already apparent in Venice in 1645 by a report by the Englishman, John Evelyn.

> This night, having with my Lord Bruce taken our places before, we went to the Opera, where comedies and other plays are represented in recitative music, by the most excellent musicians, vocal and instrumental, with variety of scenes painted and contrived with no less art of perspective, and machines for flying in the air, and other wonderful notions; taken together, it is one of the most magnificent and expensive diversions the wit of man can invent. The history was, Hercules in Lydia; the scenes changed thirteen times. The famous voices, Anna Rencia, a Roman, and reputed the best treble of women; but there was a eunuch who, in my opinion, surpassed her ...[1]

Venice alone had seven different theaters for opera by the end of the seventeenth century and between 1662 and 1680 nearly one hundred different operas were heard there.[2] There is an interesting contemporary account of opera in Venice, written by a canon of St. Mark's, Cristoforo Ivanovich, in 1681.[3] He mentions the fact that opera in Venice is public and not part of the private world of the aristocrat. He compares the construction of modern theaters with those of ancient Rome, pointing out that instead of tiers there are now private boxes. In the middle section, however, 'benches are rented out on a day-to-day basis without social distinc-

---

[1] John Evelyn, *Diary* (London, 1907), I, 202.
[2] A comprehensive description of opera in Venice is given in Lorenzo Bianconi, *Music in the Seventeenth Century*, trans. David Bryant (Cambridge: Cambridge University Press, 1987), 180ff.
[3] Quoted in Ibid., 303ff.

tion.' His description of opera in Venice in 1681 is another vivid testimonial to the decline of the original opera ideal of seeking to recreate Greek Tragedy and gives the reader a clear view of the nature of this new entertainment medium.

> The appearance of ingenious machines, as suggested by the drama, combines with the costumes and scenic display in a way which proves extremely attractive and which fully satisfies the universal curiosity aroused. In this way, lifelike elephants and real-life camels have been seen to walk the stage, as also grandiose chariots drawn by horses or other wild beasts; other sights include flying horses, dancing horses, the most magnificent machines represented by air, earth and sea with fantastic contrivances and laudable invention, to the point at which royal apartments, illuminated as for night, have been seen to descend from the air with the entire company of actors and instrumentalists, and then to return whence they came, with the great admiration of all.

As part of the changes which have occurred, he mentions the dawn of the new 'star' system and the,

> remuneration of the singers, the pretensions of these men and women having reached excessive levels (where earlier they were happy to perform irrespective of gain, or at most for honest recognition).

Being a prince of the Church, and thus associated with the noble class, he has one more worry.

> The low price charged at the entrance reduces the means available to meet the considerable cost of the pomp and display, facilitates access on the part of the ignorant and tumultuous masses and lowers the dignity of that very virtue which exists no less for delight than for profit.

One visiting diplomat was amazed to find performances of opera continuing in Venice even in times of war.[4]

A French visitor in Venice at the end of the century suggests that Venetian opera was in decline. On the other hand, his final comment is a testimonial to the great popularity of Italian opera.

> It is undeniable matter of fact, that the ornaments of those here fall extremely short of [Parisian operas]: the habits are poor, no dances, and commonly no machines, nor any illuminations, only some candles here and there, which deserve not to be mentioned. It is dangerous not to magnify the Italian music, or to say, at least, anything against it.[5]

Joseph Addison, visiting in 1701, was more impressed with opera in Venice, although he found it somewhat ridiculous 'to hear one of the rough old Romans squeaking through the mouth of a eunuch.'[6]

---

4 He is quoted in Ellen Rosand, 'Venice, 1580–1680,' *The Early Baroque Era* (Englewood Cliffs: Prentice Hall, 1994), 90.

5 F. M. Misson, *A New Voyage to Italy* (London, 1695), I, 191ff.

6 Joseph Addison, *Remarks on Several Parts of Italy in 1701* (London, 1705), 96ff.

But it is a report in 1715 by a visiting German, Uffenbach, which really gives us a view of the public itself and its behavior now that opera had become an entertainment event. This account, by the way, refers to an opera performance in which Vivaldi conducted.

> For fear of being maltreated and covered with spit as on the previous occasion, we took a box, not very expensive, and we had our revenge in behaving in relation to the people below as people had to us, a thing which previously would have seemed impossible to me … The singers were incomparable.[7]

This same behavior is documented five years later by a visiting Englishman.

> There are no open galleries, as in London, but the whole from bottom to top is all divided into boxes, which one with another will contain about six persons each. They have a scandalous custom [in Venice] of spitting out of the upper boxes, as well as throwing parings of apples or oranges, upon the company in the pit, which they do at random, without any regard where it falls; though it sometimes happens upon some of the best quality; who, though they have boxes of their own, will often come into the pit, either for the better seeing of the company, or sometimes to be nearer the stage, for the better hearing of some favorite songs.[8]

This same visitor also mentions that some listeners bring their own copies of the libretto, which they read with the help of 'wax candles in their hands.' The candles, unfortunately, 'are frequently put out by the [spit] from above.'

Italian opera, as it spread throughout Europe, carried with it the first celebrity singers, who became the daily topic of discussion in newspapers and by the public. A confrontation between the supporters of two of these provides us with another insight into the public behavior during the performance of Baroque opera.

One of these prima donnas, Francesca Cuzzoni (1700–1770) is also remembered for a rehearsal for her appearance in Handel's *Ottone*, when she declared that she disliked the aria, 'Falsa immagine,' and refused to sing it. She quickly changed her mind when Handel threatened to throw her out a window.

The other soprano was Faustina Bordoni (1700–1781), born to a noble Italian family, one which previously governed the Venetian Republic. Famous for what Charles Burney called 'a new kind of singing, by running improvisation with a neatness and velocity which astonished all who heard her,' she was heard by Handel, who took her to London for a production of his *Alessandro* in 1726.

The London audience, however, quickly took sides, some becoming supporters of Bordoni and some of Cuzzoni, and began to compete in the applause and boos they awarded their favorite. During a performance of Bononcini's *Astianatte*, in 1727, when Bordoni tried to sing, the supporters of Cuzzoni rose up in a chorus of hisses, boos, and roars. A fight broke out in

---

7 Quoted in Kendall, *Vivaldi* (London: Granada Publishing, 1979), 97.

8 Ibid., 110.

the pit and soon, on the stage itself, the two sopranos began to fight and tear each other's hair while the spectators smashed the scenery! This great competition was satirized by Gay in his *The Beggar's Opera* of 1728.[9]

There is another testimonial to the decay of opera by the great poet and librettist, Pietro Metastasio (1698–1782), who expressed his concern for the direction of Italian opera in a letter of 1750.

> In Italy, at present, there is a taste for nothing but extravagance, and vocal symphonies; in which we sometimes hear an excellent violin, flute or oboe; but never the singing of a human creature. So that music is now to excite no other emotion than that of surprise. Things are carried to such excess, that if not soon reformed, we shall justly become the buffoons of all other nations. Composers and performers being only ambitious of tickling the ear, without ever thinking of the hearts of the audience, are generally condemned in all theaters, to the disgraceful office of degrading the acts of an opera, into *intermezzi* for the dances, which occupy the attention of the people, and chief part of the spectators.[10]

Metastasio was all the more sensitive to this decay in the aesthetic aim of the theater for he had been witness to an earlier period in which the audience wept in response to the singing on the stage.[11]

Before we leave Italy we must mention that there was one musical authority who was very much in the tradition of the old philosophers. The famous singing teacher, Tosi, warned his students against being influenced by the public, observing, 'a student must not hope for applause, if he has not an utter abhorrence of ignorance.'[12] In a similar comment he states,

> It is a folly in a singer to grow vain at the first applause, without reflecting whether they are given by chance, or out of flattery; and if he thinks he deserves them, there is the end of him.[13]

The ancient philosophers had commented much on the relative values of the upper and lower classes. The general argument was that if it was something the masses liked, it must be bad. The reverse was also argued, which was the point of another observation about the public by Tosi,

> Ignorance hates all that is excellent.[14]

---

[9] Bordini married the famous German composer Johann Adolf Hasse and followed him to Dresden where they lived in happiness for thirty years, before retiring to Venice. Cuzzoni, passing through the Netherlands after she had lost her voice, was thrown into prison for her debts. By giving performances for the governor of the prison, she gradually repaid her debt and made her way to Bologna. There, in extreme poverty and squalor, she supported herself by making buttons.

[10] Letter to Farinelli, August 1, 1750, in Charles Burney, *Memoirs of the Life and Writings of the Abate Metastasio* (New York: Da Capo Press, 1971), I, 375ff. His *Clemenza di Tito* was the libretto for Mozart's opera.

[11] Letter of 1731, in Ibid., 75.

[12] P. F. Tosi, *Observations on the Florid Song* (London: Wilcox, 1743), VI, xxiii.

[13] Ibid., IX, xxii.

[14] Ibid., VII, 122.

We don't find much comment on the public by German writers, but if Johann Mattheson (1681–1764), a very prolific writer on a wide variety of musical subjects, an experienced singer, performer on organ and harpsichord and respected composer, was representative, the view must have been more like the ancient philosophers. In one place, Mattheson finds that there are two things the artist must simply accept, the ignorance and poor taste of the general public and the fact that good musicians are not well paid.[15]

There is some commentary from France which suggests that the great popularity of Italian opera, with its emphasis on entertainment, had created to some degree an environment in which the public was no longer confident about how to respond in the theater. We find this, for example, in a work by Jean de La Bruyere (1645–1696), his famous book, *Characters*.

> Why is it that we laugh so freely at the theater and yet are ashamed to weep there? Is it less natural to be moved by what is pitiful than to be amused by what is ridiculous? Are we deterred by the fear of distorting our features? Such distortion is greater in excessive laughter than in the bitterest grief, and we avert our faces to laugh as well as to weep in the presence of the great and of all those whom we respect … The extreme violence we do to our feelings by restraining our tears, and the false laughter with which we try to conceal them, clearly proves that the natural effect of great tragedy should be to make us all weep quite openly, with one accord, in other another's presence, with no further concern than to wipe our eyes; moreover, after having agreed to indulge in tears, we might discover that we generally run less risk of weeping in the theater than of dying of boredom there.[16]

There is a very similar observation by one of his contemporaries and one of France's great playwrights of the Baroque, Jean Racine (1639–1699). In the prologue to his play, *The Litigants*, his only comedy, he observes,

> Most people care not a fig for the intention or the diligence of authors. My trifle was immediately scrutinized as closely as a tragedy. Even those who had laughed the loudest trembled lest they had not laughed according not the rules, and took it ill that I had not thought more earnestly of the proper way to make them laugh. Others fancied that it was correct for them to be bored, and that the affairs of the Law Courts could not possibly furnish fit matter for the amusement of the nobility. The play was soon after performed at Versailles. There the highest in the land did not hesitate to laugh; and those who had imagined it to be disreputable to laugh in Paris, were perhaps compelled to laugh at Versailles to save their reputations.

One French writer of the Baroque really stands alone in welcoming the judgment of the public and he was Jean-Baptiste Poquelin (1622–1673), known as Molière. But, one must remember that Moliere, as a great comic playwright, was very popular in Paris, so it was easy for him to place his trust in the public. As he observes in the Preface of his *The Impertinents*,

> I refer myself to the sentence of the Multitude, and I think it as hard to oppose a work which the Public approves, as it is to defend one which it condemns.

---

15 Johann Mattheson, *Das Neu-Eröffnete Orchestre* (Hamburg, 1713), 2ff.

16 La Bruyere, *Characters*, trans. Jean Stewart (Baltimore: Penguin Books, 1970), 35ff.

In another place, Molière claims that it was the public's approval which convinced him that one of his works was in fact a good play, a claim we do not believe for a moment. In any case, in the Preface of his *The Affected Ladies*, after observing that one of his plays has been published without his knowledge, he concludes,

> Not that I intend here to play the bashful author and depreciate my own comedy out of delicacy. I should inconsistently offend all Paris if I accused it of having applauded a senseless thing; for as the public is the supreme judge of all these kinds of works, it would be impertinence in me to question its judgment; and had I entertained the worst opinion in the world of my comedy before it was acted, I am now bound to believe it to be worth something, since so many people have agreed to speak in its favor.

His appreciation of praise is voiced by a character in his *The School for Wives Criticized* (scene vi), when the playwright, Lysidas, speaks for Molière.

> LYSIDAS. I am rather late, Madam, but I had to read my play at the house of the marchioness of whom I spoke to you; and the praises bestowed upon it kept me an hour longer than I expected.
> ELISE. Praise has magic power to detain an author.

In another scene (v) in this same play, however, there is a hint that perhaps Molière had private doubts about the public. Chevalier Dorante comments on both the lower and upper class audience members at the theater, including a specific reference to musical concerts.

> Speaking generally, I would place considerable confidence in the approval of the pit, for, among those who frequent it, there are several who are capable of criticizing a play by the accepted canons, and the remainder form their opinion in the right way, which is to see things as they are, without blind prejudice, or affected compliance, or ridiculous refinement …
>
> It angers me to see these people make themselves ridiculous, in spite of their rank; they are so conceited that they are continually talking boldly of everything, no matter how ignorant they may be. They shout applause at the worst passages of a play, and never cheer those that are good; and, when they see a picture, or hear a concert, blame and praise just in the same wrong-headed way.

Pierre de Marivaux (1688–1763), a minor playwright and novelist, once took the same position regarding the value of the public's judgment as did Molière. In his *Money Makes the World Go Round*, he concludes with a *Divertissement*[17] which asks,

> The audience, we admit, knows best.
>   Have we, we wonder, passed the test?

In another play, however, Marivaux, takes quite a different view, warning the artist of the moral danger in valuing the judgment of the public.

---

[17] Marivaux's *The False Servant* also concludes with a *Divertissement* which includes singing and dance.

> We are generally more jealous of the vain applause and consideration of the multitude than desirous of the value and esteem of the wise and thinking few and, consequently, not enough solicitous after our own integrity, the only true honor.[18]

François Marie Arouet (1694–1778), known as Voltaire,[19] was the son of a successful attorney and a lively and intelligent woman who hosted a minor salon in Paris. His father advised him, 'Literature is the profession of the man who wishes to be useless to society and a burden to his relatives, and to die of hunger.' The son responded by becoming one of the most prolific writers of the Baroque, supporting his family and dying wealthy. His works include drama, poetry, history, fiction and above all philosophy.

Voltaire arrived in Paris in 1715 as France was in transition from the era of Louis XIV to the regency for the young Louis XV. His brilliant wit, and sharp tongue, soon brought him to the attention of high society and earned him several visits to the Bastille. One comment remembered from this time followed an announcement that the regent, for reasons of the economy, had sold half the horses of the royal stables. Voltaire suggested it might have been better if he dismissed half the asses at court!

One finds in Voltaire a gradual disillusionment with the public. He began to question whether even the contributions of the great playwrights, Corneille and Molière, had any lasting effect. In the Preface to his play, *Catiline*, Voltaire writes,

> What progress those arts may have made in France, those gentlemen of distinguished genius and abilities who have cultivated them among us have not yet imparted true taste to the whole nation. We are not born so happy as the Greeks and Romans, but frequent the theater more out of idleness than from any real regard to literature.[20]

His outlook for the theater was increasingly dark. In his dedication of *Orestes* to the duchess of Maine, Voltaire concludes,

> All that I wish for, Madam, is, that some genius may be found to finish what I have but just sketched out; to free the stage from that effeminacy and affectation which it is now sunk into; to render it respectable to the gravest characters.[21]

In a letter to a friend in 1775, Voltaire sees only a dismal end to French taste in music as well as in the theater.

---

[18] Marivaux, *The Virtuous Orphan*, trans. Mary Collyer (Carbondale: Southern Illinois University Press, 1965), 66.
[19] He took the name Voltaire, a name which had been in his mother's family, while in the Bastille.
[20] Quoted in *The Works of Voltaire* (New York: St. Hubert Guild, 1901), X IX, 261ff.
[21] Quoted in Ibid., XVII, 67ff.

> Nothing is so sacred that it is not abused. We are going to lapse into the extravagant and the gigantic in all things. Farewell to beautiful verse; farewell to feelings of the heart; farewell to everything. Music will soon be nothing more than an Italian din, and theatrical plays nothing more than conjurer's tricks. They wanted to improve everything, but everything has degenerated.[22]

At the end of his life, reflecting on the decay of theater in Paris, he writes,

> I have seen the end of the reign of reason and taste.[23]

And finally, there was disillusionment with the public, whom Voltaire has Ismenia refer to in his, *Merope* (IV, v), as,

> the fickle crowd, still fond of novelty.

Voltaire advises 'dread the public' in the dedication of his *The Orphan of China*, when he quotes an anonymous Chinese author:

> When you compose any work, show it only to your friends; dread the public, and your brother writers; for they will play false with you, abuse everything you do, and impute to you what you never did: calumny with her hundred trumpets, will sound them all to your destruction; whilst truth, who is dumb, shall remain with you.[24]

The final dissolution with the environment for theater in Paris, for Voltaire, came when his close friend, the actress Adrienne le Couvreur (1692–1730) was denied burial on church property because she was an actress. In a rage, Voltaire wrote his poem, 'La Mort de Mademoiselle Le Couvreur.'

> They deprive of burial,
> Her who in Greece would have had altars.
> I have seen them adoring her, crowding about her;
> Hardly is she dead when she becomes a criminal!

Upon the death of Voltaire, he too was refused a Christian burial by the Archbishop of Paris and so was secretly buried by his friends. Shortly after the beginning of the Revolution he was reburied with great ceremony in Paris, following a processional led by Lafayette and a performance of Gossec's *Patriotic Chorus*, W. 83, for chorus and band.

In England we find a very interesting work by John Playford (1623–1686), in the preface to his *Introduction to the Skill of Music* of 1674. In addition to his reference to the public as 'the ignorant vulgar,' he documents his own attempts to compose in the new Italian fashion. For

---

[22] Letter to Charles-Augustin Feriol (October, 1769), in *The Selected Letters of Voltaire*, trans. Richard Brooks (New York: New York University Press, 1973), 285.

[23] Letter to Charles Augustin Feriol (July, 1775), in *Select Letters of Voltaire*, trans. Theodore Besterman (London: Nelson, 1963), 174.

[24] Dedication to Richelieu, of *The Orphan of China*, in *The Works of Voltaire*, XV, 180.

him it was all for nothing as his music was lost in improvisation. He objects especially to the English habit of playing 'divisions,' a very square, repetitive, sequential and unmusical form of elaboration.

> But I have endeavored in those my late compositions, to bring in a kind of music, by which men might as it were talk in harmony, using in that kind of singing a certain noble neglect of the song (as I have often heard at Florence by the actors in their singing operas) in which I endeavored the imitation of the conceit of the words, seeking out the chords more or less passionate … But, as I said before, those long windings and turnings of the voice are ill used, for I have observed that divisions have been invented, not because they are necessary unto a good fashion of singing, but rather for a certain tickling of the ears of those who do not well understand what it is to sing passionately; for if they did, undoubtedly divisions would have been abhorred, there being nothing more contrary to passion than they are … Whereas those that well understand the conceit and the meaning of the words…and can distinguish where the passion is more or less required. Which sort of people we should endeavor to please with all diligence, and more to esteem their praise, than the applause of the ignorant vulgar.[25]

Among the Puritan writers in England there were two who argued against the importance of the public with a passion reminiscent of the old philosophers. Sir Thomas Browne (1605–1682) declares the public is the enemy of reason, virtue and religion!

> If there be any among those common objects of hatred I do condemn and laugh at, it is that great enemy of reason, virtue, and religion, the multitude; that numerous piece of monstrosity, which, taken asunder, seem men, and the reasonable creatures of God, but, confused together, make but one great beast, and a monstrosity more prodigious than Hydra.[26]

And William Penn (1644–1718) for whom an American state is named, wrote of his concern for applause, which we must assume was due to religious concerns with pride and humility.

> As there is no passion in us sooner moved, or more deceivable, so for that reason there is none over which we ought to be more watchful, whether we give or receive it: for if we give it, we must be sure to mean it, and measure it too.
>
> ……
>
> It is much easier for him to merit applause, than hear of it: and he never doubts himself more, or the person that gives it, than when he hears so much of it.[27]

Finally, in William Shenstone (1714–1763), a minor figure in English literature, we find a convert to the movement toward entertainment in the theater. He can see nothing at all wrong with the artist who seeks to be popular.

> I cannot see why people are ashamed to acknowledge their passion for popularity. The love of popularity is the love of being beloved …
> I am afraid humility to genius is as an extinguisher to a candle.[28]

---

[25] John Playford, *An Introduction to the Skill of Music* [1674] (Ridgewood: Gregg Press, 1966), preface.
[26] *Sir Thomas Browne's Works*, ed. Simon Wilkin (London: Pickering, 1836), II, 86.
[27] *The Select Works of William Penn* (London: William Phillips, 1825), III, 401.
[28] William Shenstone, *Men and Manners* (Boston: Houghton Mifflin, 1927), 51.

The Nineteenth-Century Artist and the Public

Popularity, the curse of every grand and noble thing.[1]
Richard Wagner

THIS ESSAY IS THE FOURTH IN A SERIES dedicated to considering the advice of past philosophers on the relationship of the artist to his public. Those who have read the first three essays have seen a unanimous consent, across two thousand years, that the composer or artist must not write or program for the masses. While their reasons varied, their implied advice was that to do so was to lose one's integrity as an artist, to lose one's soul.

By the nineteenth century we find the greatest musicians also addressing this topic. These views are worthy of much reflection as their music is still at the heart of our regular repertoire and their views very much apply to our time. Robert Schumann, in 1840, writes of the cost so often mentioned by the ancient writers, that of losing one's soul.

> The merely mechanical artist unfortunately often loses, in the tumult of the world, his most priceless possession—that ingenuous, unaffected, cheerful art-power which he sacrifices to the lower demands of the masses, until it is completely buried under the commonplace routine of life.[2]

In his role as a critic, Schumann wrote of this problem with respect to the composer, Reissiger, a man whom he regarded as having real potential. Schumann regretted that Reissiger tended to write common passages 'that secure speedy applause from the public.'

> Who is not pleased with applause? But the praise of the stricter critic, whose glance ever seeks the noblest in art … would also be granted, were it not for the too visible thirst for applause.[3]

One senses that Schumann was confused why a man of such obvious talent would make this choice. It was a choice which equally confounded Richard Wagner, who observed,

> The passion for publicity is hard to comprehend: each experience teaches that it is an evil sphere.[4]

The great composer, Felix Mendelssohn, was very well aware of this choice which every artist must make and he took his stand firmly against writing for the public and expressed this conviction repeatedly.

---

1 'A Happy Evening,' in *Richard Wagner's Prose Works*, trans. William Ashton Ellis (New York: Broude), VII, 74
2 'Alexis Lwoff,' in *Neue Zeitschrift für Musik*, 1840.
3 'Chamber Music,' in *Neue Zeitschrift für Musik*, 1837.
4 'The Artist and Publicity,' in *Richard Wagner's Prose Works* (New York: Broude), VII, 136.

> An upright man has the hardest stand to make, in knowing that the public are more attracted by outward show than by truth.[5]
>
> ......
>
> If I am not adapted for popularity, I will not try to acquire it, nor seek after it; and if you think this wrong, then I ought rather to say I *cannot* seek after it, for really I *cannot*, but would not if I could.[6]
>
> ......
>
> Ever since I began to compose, I have remained true to my starting principle: not to write a page because no matter what public, or what pretty girl wanted it to be thus or thus; but to write solely as I myself thought best, and as it gave me pleasure. I will not depart from this principle in writing an opera, and this makes it so very hard, since most people, as well as most poets, look upon an opera merely as a thing to be popular.[7]

The foregoing comments had to do with the 'bottom line,' does one elect to pander to the public at the expense of one's soul. Behind those comments there had no doubt been much thought given to the underlying aesthetic question of 'pleasing the audience.' It must have been a question frequently discussed for Schumann seems truly exasperated when he writes,

> People say, 'It pleased;' or 'It did not please.' As if there were nothing higher than the art of *pleasing* the public![8]

His own personal position as a young artist was very clear. In 1832 he wrote, 'I have no desire to be understood by the common herd'[9] and in 1840,

> The applause of a fashionable mob is not worth the esteem of one quiet, true, exclusive artist.[10]

But he grieved that his fellow German composers often made the wrong choice, indeed believing that there was a certain paradox involved: the more one tries to be popular, the less one is.

> German composers usually fail on account of their desire of pleasing the public. But let any one of them only give us something original, simple, deeply, spontaneously and inwardly felt, and he will soon find that he can accomplish more in such a manner. The public is apt to turn a cold shoulder to the man who is perpetually opening his arms to it. Beethoven walked around with bent head and folded arms; the crowd shrank away timidly, but gradually became familiar with, and fond of, his extraordinary speech.[11]

---

5   Letter to Conrad Schleinitz, August 1, 1838.
6   Letter to Ferdinand David, July 30, 1838.
7   Letter to Eduard Devrient, June 28, 1843.
8   Robert Schumann's Diary, ca. 1833.
9   Letter to his mother, August 9, 1832.
10 'Trios,' in *Neue Zeitschrift für Musik*, 1840.
11 'German Opera,' in *Neue Zeitschrift für Musik*, 1842.

It is interesting that after he had a family, Schumann softened his position somewhat, or so he suggests in a private letter of 1843.

> I used to be indifferent to the amount of notice I received, but a wife and children put a different complexion upon everything. It becomes imperative to think of the future, desirable to see the fruits of one's labor—not the artistic, but the prosaic fruits necessary to life.[12]

By the end of his life, however, he was reiterating his original aesthetic principles,

> Have you also failed to glean from my music that I do not write with the sole intent to please children and amateurs?[13]

Mendelssohn, in a letter to one of his former teachers, calls himself, 'an anti-public-caring musician,'[14] but he also noticed an interesting irony,

> I have always found that those pieces which I have written with the least regard for people have pleased them best.[15]

Richard Wagner stated his fundamental aesthetic principle with regard to the public in a widely quoted definition:

> I assert that it is impossible for anything to be truly good if it is reckoned in advance for presentation to the public and this intended presentation rules the composer in his sketch and composition of an artwork.[16]

When one recalls that the final symphony of Beethoven was rarely performed until after mid-century, as it was considered too difficult to understand,[17] then one can imagine how the works of Berlioz and the first successful operas of Wagner must have astonished listeners. Wagner was then apparently often approached by young composers who mistakenly concluded that the 'great effect' was the next path. But for Wagner, this was just another way of pandering to the public.

> 'Effect,' a stunning of the spectator's senses, to be documented by the outburst of 'applause.'[18]

---

[12] Letter to Carl Kossmaly, Mary 5, 1843.
[13] Letter to J. N., Sept. 22, 1851.
[14] Letter to Ignaz and Charlotte Moscheles, June 24, 1834.
[15] Letter to Eduard Devrient, Milan, July 13, 1831.
[16] 'Public and Popularity,' in *Richard Wagner's Prose Works*, VI, 55.
[17] Before the first performance in Paris the Conservatoire Orchestra, the best in town, rehearsed the work for three years, not because they could not play it, but because they wanted to make sure they understood it.
[18] *Richard Wagner's Prose Works*, V, 133.

In another place he writes,

> I have never yet made the acquaintance of a young composer who did not think to gain my sanction for 'audacities' before all things.

His response, in this case, was to point the antithesis of 'audacious,' the utter simplicity of the beginning of his *Rheingold* in which a single chord is heard for five minutes or so. He says it was impossible for him to change this chord as he had no reason for changing it.[19]

In one place, Wagner appears to have given up hope on ever finding an audience whose primary purpose was other than to be entertained.

> Here reads the rule: the Public wills to be amused, and thou must seek to smuggle in thine Own beneath the mantle of Amusement.[20]

And so we return to the choice, is one going to be an artist or please the public. But, one might argue, is it not possible to have it both ways? Both Schumann and Wagner gave a resounding, 'No,' to this question. Schumann's observation came as he was writing about Viennese composers.

> The same thing has been said, with the same result, of a hundred other Viennese composers; they want one thing, yet cannot give up the other; they must be artists, and yet please the crowd; boundless failures in this endeavor have not yet opened their eyes to the fact that nothing can be attained on such a path; that only one aim leads to an end, and to reach that, we must fulfill our duty to ourselves and to art.[21]

Wagner illustrated the choice open to the young artist in a vivid and memorable metaphor,

> To take a last look back upon the picture afforded us by the Public, we might compare it with a river, as to which we must decide whether we will swim against or with its stream. Who swims with it, may imagine he belongs to constant progress; 'tis so easy to be borne along, and he never notes that he is being swallowed in the ocean of vulgarity. To swim against the stream, must seem ridiculous to those not driven by an irresistible force to the immense exertions that it costs.[22]

The artists we have been quoting had obviously given much thought to the nature of the audience in general. In some cases they concluded that the public really did not understand great music. Liszt thought that in the case of Chopin not only was the public incapable of understanding his sophisticated music but that Chopin was quite aware of this fact.

---

[19] Ibid., VI, 185.
[20] 'The Artist and Publicity,' in Ibid., VII, 136.
[21] 'Trios for Pianoforte, Violin and Violoncello,' in *Neue Zeitschrift für Musik*, 1842.
[22] *Richard Wagner's Prose Works*, VI, 94.

> Chopin knew that he had no effect upon the multitude and could not strike the masses … He knew that he was completely appreciated only in those too rare gatherings where all the hearers were ready to follow and accompany him into those spheres that the ancients entered solely through an ivory gate surrounded by diamond pilasters crowned by domes …
>
> Aware of the conditions imposed by the nature of his talent, he played but rarely in public … His voluntary sacrifice of clamorous success concealed an internal hurt. He had a very clear sense of his great superiority, but perhaps its echo and reverberation did not suffice to bring him the quiet certainly that he was fully appreciated. Popular acclamation was lacking, and he doubtless wondered to what degree the distinguished salons compensated, in the enthusiasm of their applause, for the general public that he avoided.[23]

Schumann believed that any music which was out of the ordinary would not be understood by the audience.

> The characteristic of the extraordinary is, that it cannot always be understood; the majority understand best what is superficial-virtuoso music, for example.[24]

Wagner felt that every audience was a mixture of interested listeners and those who had no interest at all and that he had found no way of predicting which listener was which on any basis of societal judgment. Of this he provides a touching example:

> What brought them here may certainly be gauged as nothing but the quest of entertainment, and that in the case of every comer … Nor are the various grades of society and education, to which the spectators belong, by any means an index to the individual's receptiveness: in the dearest, as in the cheapest seats, one meets the same phenomenon of interest and apathy packed side by side. At one of the excellent first performances of *Tristan* in Munich I observed a vigorous dame of middle age in the last extremity of boredom during the third act, while the cheeks of her husband, a grey-beard superior officer, were streaming with tears of the deepest emotion.[25]

Franz Liszt was once encouraged by the public's response to Wagner's *Tannhauser*,[26] but often he doubted the understanding and only found a kind of societal demand to applaud,

> they will think themselves in honor bound to admire and applaud what they cannot understand.[27]

Schumann found that such polite applause was particularly evident when early music was performed.

---

23 Franz Liszt, *Frederic Chopin* (Paris: Escudier, 1852).
24 Robert Schumann's Diary, ca. 1833.
25 'Public and Popularity,' in *Richard Wagner's Prose Works*, VI, 63.
26 Letter to Richard Wagner, Jan. 14, 1850.
27 Letter to Richard Wagner, Sept. 2, 1850.

> A great many people conducted themselves as if they thought we were doing Bach an honor, as if we were wiser than the olden time, and thought it all both curious and interesting! The connoisseurs were the worst of all, smiling as if Bach had written for them—he who could have swung us all, together or separately, on his little finger—Handel, too ... Or Gluck, not less so. And people listen, praise, and think no more about it.[28]

The thought had no doubt presented itself that this was a matter of *educating* the public and that perhaps the great composers should take a more active role in this. Schumann, for one, had concluded that there was not the slightest hope for success in educating the public.

> We have, of course, not the slightest hope or thought of teaching the masses to understand the difference between composition and conglomeration, between the life of a master and apparent life.[29]

Liszt believed that the public's taste in music was formed only by reading the newspapers.[30] For this reason, reflecting a public school system still characterized by corporal punishment, he contended that the artists must educate the public and if necessary through violence and a good beating!

> It is not only the singers and the orchestras that must be brought up to the mark to serve as instruments in the *dramatic revolution*, ... but also, and before all, the *public*, which must be elevated to a level where it becomes capable of associating itself by sympathy and intelligent comprehension with conceptions of a higher order than that of the lazy amusements with which it feeds its imagination and sensibility at our theaters every day. This must be done, if need be, by violence, for, as the Gospel tells us, the kingdom of heaven suffers violence, and only those who use violence will take it ...
>
> The enemy to whom, as you, my great art-hero, rightly put it, one should not capitulate—that enemy is not only in the throats of the singers, but also very essentially in the lazy and at the same time tyrannical habits of the hearers. On these as well as on the others one must make an impression if necessary by a good beating.[31]

Liszt also had a specific repertoire in mind that the public must learn,

> The *Panis Angelicus*, by Palestrina, the Schumann *Quintet* and the sublime Prelude to *Lohengrin* are works which a well-brought-up public ought to know by heart.[32]

Wagner agreed the public must be educated by the artists themselves, but through a much more subtle process.

> I believe an audience should never be criticized: it will always retain the sovereignty of a child. How should it be reproached for its taste? After all, it fails utterly and completely to hear or see what strikes us artists as being essential. It clings to the events on stage, and to nothing else, but in these

---

[28] 'A Retrospective View of Musical Life in Leipzig during the Winder of 1837–1838,' in *Neue Zeitschrift für Musik*, 1838.
[29] 'Etudes for the Pianoforte,' in *Neue Zeitschrift für Musik*, 1839.
[30] Letter to Johann von Hrbeck, March 3, 1875.
[31] Letter to Richard Wagner, Sept. 16, 1850.
[32] Letter to Jessie Laussot, Jan. 13, 1868.

> it takes a wholly personal interest: but of all that lies behind these events and which we ourselves consider the only true object of art, it knows not a thing. And herein lies our entire consolation: for we can hope to present *ourselves* and our higher aims behind these events on stage; and in that way we shall persuade our audiences, by means of the correct illusion, to acquire, without noticing it, a greater refinement of taste.[33]

In his essay, 'On Poetry and Composition,' Wagner discusses the influence on public taste which is due to the publishers. In a comment that should be very familiar to music educators today, he wrote, 'It is just this perpetual output of rubbish that hoists the publisher to eminence.'[34]

In another place Wagner felt programming confused the audience, giving the illustration of having works by Bach or Mozart set next to contemporary music.[35] He also argued for *only* having pure art music performed before the public. There should be nothing performed which was composed with a purpose[36] or anything written 'to please' the audience, which must be considered morally bad.[37]

Just like those centuries of their earlier colleagues, these composers had a very dim view of the character of their public. For Schumann, the character of the audience could be read in their faces while they listened to the performance.

> If you wish to understand a man, you ask him who are his friends; if you want to judge a public, you observe what it applauds, what sort of a physiognomy it presents after listening to music.[38]

For Liszt the audience was an almost immovable force:

> They are like a sea of lead and no less heavy to move, their waves are stirred by fire. They need the strong arm of the stalwart laborer to be spilled into a mold where the flowing metal suddenly assumes thought and feeling in accordance with the imposed form.[39]

The main reason for this, he once wrote, was the generally poor background in high quality music.

---

33 Letter to Hans von Bulow, Dec. 27, 1868.
34 *Richard Wagner's Prose Works*, VI, 133ff.
35 Ibid., IV, 201ff.
36 Ibid., IV, 107.
37 Ibid., VI, 67.
38 Robert Schumann's Diary, ca. 1833.
39 Liszt, *Chopin*, 1852.

> In our stupid musical customs, often very anti-musical, it is almost impossible to appeal to a badly informed public by a second performance immediately after the first; and at Leipzig, as elsewhere, one only meets with a very small number of people who know how to apply cause and effect intelligently and enthusiastically to a piece out of the common, and signed with the name of a composer who is not dead.[40]

Liszt was particularly disturbed in the fact that the newspapers had such a strong influence on the opinion of the public. He pointed, by way of example, to a concert in Vienna in 1884.

> The Vienna performance of Sgambati's Symphony was fairly well received but in the *Presse*, Hanslick was critical. Hence it is a failure. The public is easily discouraged by a newspaper article.[41]

He once found some ironic satisfaction in seeing a large audience which was the result of a printing error in a local newspaper.

> A well-known piece of Bazzini's, 'La Ronde des Lutins,' was by a printer's error, called 'Ronde des Cretins!' ['Rondo of Idiots']. What an immeasurable large public for such a Rondo![42]

Again, his principal concern, of course, was the role the papers played in forming the consensus public view. In 1869, he observed,

> People know pretty well what to think by what they hear said, without any need of hearing the works.[43]

He regretted that society was now flocking to see opera,

> Nowadays, more than ever, the public thirst for Opera alone. Everything else in music is nonsense to them,[44]

with the result that everything else found little interest.

> Alas! Everything that is not of the *theater* and does not belong to the repertoire of the old classical masters Handel, Bach, Palestrina, etc., does not yet gain any attentive and paying consideration—the decisive criterion–of the public. Berlioz during his life time, furnished the proof of this.[45]

As for Wagner, his characterization of the general public which he found in the theater was just a very bored group of people.

---

[40] Letter to Anton Rubinstein, Nov. 19, 1854.
[41] Letter to Olga von Meyendorff, Feb. 3, 1884.
[42] Letter to Felix Draseke, Jan. 10, 1858.
[43] Letter to Franz Servais, Dec. 20, 1869.
[44] Letter to Eduard Liszt, June 6, 1878.
[45] Letter to Malwine Tardieu, March 6, 1883.

> The places in our halls of entertainment are mostly filled by nothing but that section of our citizen society whose only ground for change of occupation is utter 'boredom': the disease of boredom, however, is not remediable by sips of Art; for it can never be distracted of set purpose, but merely duped into another form of boredom.[46]

These great composers also left some comments about specific audiences which the reader may find interesting. Schumann found Vienna a town inclined toward entertainment. In characterizing the artist who tried to go a different direction he employs the same 'river metaphor' used by Wagner, above.

> Public and publishers in Vienna desire above all things light and entertaining, and a firework exhibition suits them better than a robust gladiator. So it has often happened that those who did not understand this, but struggled against the stream, have been obliged to do so alone and unapplauded; while those who abandoned their higher aim and yielded swam with a hundred others in the current, and disappeared without leaving a trace behind them.[47]

Liszt found a similar disinterest in art music in Munich.

> The Munich public is more or less neutral, more observing and listening than sympathetic. The Court does not take the slightest interest in music.[48]

Some thought Paris to be the center of the musical world for most of the nineteenth century. Certainly every artist had to perform there, but Mendelssohn found that music in this country was primarily only a curiosity.

> The public at these [Conservatoire] concerts also loves Beethoven devotedly because it believes one has to be a connoisseur in order to love him; but only the fewest can take genuine pleasure in him, and I simply cannot bear to listen to people depreciating Haydn and Mozart; it makes me wild. The Beethoven symphonies to them are a kind of exotic plant, people sniff at their perfume but look upon them as curiosities.[49]

Wagner found appreciative audiences in Paris, so long as the music was such as to be predestined for the audience to like it.

> For every genre they cultivate a special theater; this theater is frequented by those to whom that genre appeals: and thus it comes that, apart from all intrinsic worth of their productions, the French invariably turn out good work, namely homogeneous stage performances presented to a homogeneous audience.[50]

---

[46] *Richard Wagner's Prose Works*, III, 96.
[47] 'Trios,' in *Neue Zeitschrift für Musik*, 1840.
[48] Leltter to Richard Wagner, Dec. 25, 1856.
[49] Letter to Carl Zelter, Paris, Feb. 15, 1832.
[50] 'Public and Popularity,' in *Richard Wagner's Prose Works*, VI, 64.

Mendelssohn was extraordinarily popular in England (and still is) and this unusual success is often mentioned by his somewhat envious rivals. Even though Mendelssohn thought it 'necessity in every foreign city of playing so as to make myself understood by the audience,'[51] he nevertheless found the reaction in England to his music to be somewhat strange.

> I have never before achieved such a decided effect with my music as in Birmingham, and have never seen the public so entirely taken up with me alone. And yet there is something about it—what shall I call it—something flighty and evanescent, which depressed and frightens rather than encourages me.[52]

Finally, while the audience behavior does not seem to have been as bad as the reader saw in the case of Italian opera during the Baroque, nevertheless there are two references which may be of interest. Schumann must have had some noisy audiences, for he dreamed of playing for the deaf and dumb!

> So, my public ... How long have I not desired to found concerts for the deaf and dumb, to set you an example of good behavior, of which you display little, even in the finest concerts![53]

In the essay on the audiences of the ancient world the reader read of audiences *hissing* the artist. It seems odd that Liszt should report this behavior still present in the nineteenth century in Paris.

> Pasdeloup's ... final argument that 'music must be listened to before being hissed' is reasonable. I go even further and consider that hisses are poor company: silence suffices for a well-brought-up audience to express its disapproval.[54]

The tenor of everything above has to do with a distrust of popularity and even with the audience itself. However, there is such a thing as universality, which is much discussed in the field of drama criticism, but not so much in music. Even if not discussed much, Beethoven was clearly proving the principle of universality already in the nineteenth century, the concept that an artist could compose or perform only music of the highest sophistication and still be understood by the broad public. Schumann wrote on this subject more than any other composer during the nineteenth century, but he appears ambivalent on the subject. In 1832 he writes that the public will indeed recognize any composition which is really remarkable.

> The public, which forgets so easily, seldom overlooks anything really remarkable, though I am sometimes tempted to compare it to a herd of cattle momentarily distracted by the lightning from its peaceful grazing.[55]

---

[51] Letter to his brother and sisters, Rome, Nov. 26, 1830.
[52] Letter to Ferdinand Hiller, Dec. 10, 1837.
[53] 'Letters of an Enthusiast,' in *Neue Zeitschrift für Musik*, 1835.
[54] Letter to Olga von Meyendorff, Nov. 16, 1876.
[55] Letter to Friedrich Wieck, Jan. 11, 1832.

And in following years makes similar declarations.

> A remark of yours is in my mind, about my meeting with so little appreciation. Don't be afraid, my dear Clara, you shall live to see my compositions come into notice, and be much talked about. I have no fear, and it will all get better by degrees, '*within itself.*'[56]
>
> ......
>
> A public crowd is never to be satisfied; but a carefully worked out, finely finished work of art re-echoes through centuries.[57]

On the other hand, among his writings we find two instances which clearly demonstrate a lack of faith in the principle of universality.

> Half-educated persons are generally unable to discover more than the expression of grief and joy, and perhaps melancholy, in music without words; they are deaf to the finer shades of passion—anger, revenge, satisfaction, quietude, etc. On this account, it is difficult for them to understand great masters like Schubert and Beethoven, who have translated almost every possible condition of life into the speech of tones.[58]
>
> ......
>
> Where is the composer whose fame is universal? Where is the work—were it even of Divine origin—universally acknowledged as sacred?[59]

Mendelssohn accepted the idea of universality, but only with a qualification,

> I believe that no man ever yet succeeded in controlling and commanding the minds of others by *one* work; a succession of works all aiming at one point can alone do it.[60]

One finds observations by great musicians of the twentieth century follow the same principles the reader has seen testimony to from the nineteenth century, and indeed since ancient societies, continue little changed after two thousand five hundred. Arnold Schoenberg, for example, is quoted as observing that the highest art music cannot be expected to be understood by the broad public.

> If it is art, it is not for all; and if it is for all, it is not art.[61]

And the great conductor, Antal Dorati, echoing the advice of centuries, warns that neither the composer nor the conductor should ever pander to the public.

---

56 Letter to Clara Wieck, Oct. 10, 1839.
57 'Trios,' in *Neue Zeitschrift für Musik*, 1840.
58 'On the Comic in Music,' in *Neue Zeitschrift für Musik*, 1835.
59 Letter to Franz Brendel, Sept. 18, 1849.
60 Letter to Edouard Franck, Jan. 8, 1838.
61 Quoted in Nat Shapiro, *An Encyclopedia of Quotations about Music* (New York: Da Capo Press, 1978), 237.

> Art is not a civil service … the composer does have a duty, but it is very high. It is a sacred duty. It is toward his art. The composer should not think about what pleases people.[62]

Two more recent distinguished conductors have commented on attempts to have it both ways, with the goal of pleasing the public. Felix Weingartner comments on those conductors who perform low quality music under the belief that their 'great' performance will justify the choice.

> A good performance of a poor work is of no artistic consequence, and regrettable both because it furthers bad taste and because it means time and labor unprofitably squandered.[63]

A too frequent illustration of what Weingartner was concerned with is the concert of fine literature which ends with a 'crowd pleaser,' a march or other light work. We have even had the occasion to hear such a composition as Husa's *Music for Prague*, followed by a march! The sad aesthetic fact is that such a closing work will inevitably erase from the audience's memory everything before it—just like hitting the delete key. The distinguished choral conductor, William Finn, recalled just such a sad example, a performance by a celebrated baritone, John Charles Thomas, who,

> After [the conclusion of] Verdi's *Aida*, stood before a crowded house … and sang 'Home on the Range,' to applause and cheers.[64]

Another distinguished conductor of the twentieth century, the Austrian, Peter Paul Fuchs, wrote of the need for the conductor to program the highest repertoire, even if it does not seem to reach most of the audience.

> It seems to me that there is no harm in admitting it—only a comparatively small amount of the music offered in a symphony concert reaches the hearts and minds of the audience; the rest is heard but not listened to.[65]

Bruno Walter goes further and offers an assessment of the actual injury to the public body by entertainment music.

> The cataracts of music pouring forth from radio stations and other sources day in and day out; the assimilation of musical and literary works to what is supposed to be the taste of the age; the inundation of the masses with entertainments, amusements, diversion, distractions—all this endangers the serious inner life today and spiritual aspirations of those who are exposed to it.[66]

---

[62] Richard Carter, 'An Interview with Antal Dorati,' *The Instrumentalist* (December, 1980).
[63] Felix Weingartner, *On Conducting* (New York: Kalmus), 19.
[64] William J. Finn, *The Conductor Raises his Baton* (London: Dobson, 1946), 6.
[65] Peter Paul Fuchs, *The Psychology of Conducting* (New York: MCA, 1969), 112ff.
[66] Bruno Walter, *Of Music and Music-Making* (New York: Norton, 1957), 18.

And so, where are we today? What have we learned from two thousand five hundred years of thought by the greatest thinkers of civilization? There are two fundamental lessons.

1. Every musician has the free choice to be either an artist or an entertainer.
2. He cannot be both, it is either the one or the other.

Let us begin with the first fundamental lesson. What is the difference? By art music we mean it has no purpose, other than the direct communication from composer to listener of emotional truth. Wagner wrote that only such 'objectless' music can be truly beautiful, as its nature is high above vulgar purpose and makes the 'ends of life worth following.'[67] In another place Wagner makes this a moral choice and calls entertainment music, 'morally bad in so far as it makes for profit from the most questionable attributes of the crowd.'[68]

In terms of music education, we would put it somewhat differently. We would say the music educator who chooses to be an artist makes available to his students two unique areas of personal growth potential, two areas of significant personality development.

1. He brings his students into direct one-to-one contact with some of the greatest minds who have ever lived and with spiritually noble people.
2. The school music educator can offer a curriculum centered on catharsis, through which he makes it possible for his students to explore, experience and refine more lofty feelings and emotions, to get to know themselves on this side of their personality and compare these higher feelings with their own.

With respect to his public, his job is to educate it, as Liszt pointed out:

> The word 'Evening entertainment' must, as is self-evident, be entirely dispensed with. Our business is to raise, to educate the audience, not to amuse them.[69]

The music educator who chooses to be an entertainer foregoes the above two areas of personal growth above. They are obtainable only from the highest form of classical music and are not obtainable from jazz or any other form of popular music. In giving these opportunities for personal growth, in return the educator may gain popularity. But there is a terrible price to pay for this popularity, as Wagner pointed out:

> The man who strays into the realm of triviality must pay for his transgression at the cost of his own more noble nature. He who seeks the trivial deliberately has nothing worth losing.[70]

---

[67] Quoted in *Richard Wagner's Prose Works*, IV, 107.
[68] Ibid., VI, 67.
[69] Letter to an Unknown Person, Spring, 1859.
[70] Letter to Eduard Hanslick, Jan. 1, 1847.

He has, in other words, lost his soul. This is a very real thing for which one can find testimony in two public letters. One,[71] is by a man at the end of his life who admits going into music education because of the lure of applause. He specialized in marching band and he discusses his success and the fact that no one ever questioned what he was doing. But at the end of his life he realized he was not *really* a music educator, but an entertainer. It is a very sad and touching letter to read.

The second letter is by a beginning teacher,[72] at the other end of life. She relates being dismayed as a beginning music teacher to discover that music educators are 'viewed as entertainers, not as "real" teachers.' Consequently, of course, she found that music is not considered a 'real' subject. It is another touching letter to read. These two letters describe a reality and it is a reality whose history is one of individual choice.

Now, as for the second lesson learned from all these prior philosophers, why is it we cannot have it both ways? Why must we be viewed as one or the other? The question was framed by Schumann, which we quote above, but repeat here:

> The same thing has been said, with the same result, of a hundred other Viennese composers; they want one thing, yet cannot give up the other; they must be artists, and yet please the crowd; boundless failures in this endeavor have not yet opened their eyes to the fact that nothing can be attained on such a path.

Why is this so? It is because the perception by the public will not allow it, or as Eugene Ormandy once expressed it in a private discussion with us, 'the public will not allow you to wear two hats.' It is true, and we might offer it, on the basis of centuries of evidence, as a maxim: the conductor who tries to be both will *always* be viewed as an entertainer by the public.

This is the core problem with the university band and wind ensemble movement. These conductors ask each other constantly, 'why does the public not accept us on the same level as an orchestra?' They think commissioning more composers to write music for them is the answer, but this activity has gone unnoticed by the public. They think perhaps if there were some 'professional bands' that this might be the key to open the public mind. But, again, they are wrong. The real reason the public does not accept the band on the same level as the orchestra is because the public sees the band as an entertainment medium. And it is. And *this*, the band conductors are not yet willing to give up.

---

[71] Published in *Today's Music Educator*, Fall, 1992.

[72] Published in *Band Directors Guide*, March/April, 1992.

Early Views on Criticism

For what I have published I can only hope to be pardoned;
but for what I have burned I deserve to be praised.

Alexander Pope (1688–1744)

ONE DOES NOT FIND MUCH INTERESTING DISCUSSION of criticism in the works of the ancient Greek and Roman philosophers. However, critics must have always been present and their traces can be found in two nice anecdotes recalled by Pliny the Elder (23–79 AD). One is of a painter who, weary of criticism, added a line of poetry under one of his paintings to the effect that it is easier to complain about his work than to copy it. The other story is about another painter who made the habit of standing behind his paintings when they were exhibited for the first time, in order to hear the comments of the public. He professed to profit from these remarks as he considered the public to be a more observant critic than himself. On one occasion when he heard a shoemaker object to some minor detail of a shoe he had painted, the artist actually changed the painting. The next day, hiding behind the painting again, the artist heard the same shoemaker taking pride that his criticism had resulted in the improvement of the shoe in the painting and then elevate his criticism to the leg in the painting. The artist now jumped out from behind the painting, indignantly rebuking him, saying a shoemaker's criticism should not go beyond the sandal—a remark which Pliny says became a proverb![1]

Also from the first century of the modern era we have an extraordinary treatise on aesthetics, called 'On the Sublime,' by a writer named Longinus, of whom nothing else is known. Longinus takes the sensible position that one is best served by learning to be one's own critic. How, he asks, would I hear this if I were in the audience, or, more formidable still, what would Homer think, if he were in the audience? To imagine 'great heroes, acting as judges,' does, he admits, make the 'ordeal' of speaking a 'severe one.' But now he adds 'greater incentive' by proposing the question,

> 'In what spirit will each succeeding age listen to me who have written thus?' But if one shrinks from the very thought of uttering aught that may transcend the term of his own life and time, the conceptions of his mind must necessarily be incomplete, blind, and as it were untimely born, since they are by no means brought to the perfection needed to ensure a futurity of fame.

---

[1] Pliny, *Natural History*, XXXV, xxxvi, 63 and 85, The proverb remains observed in academia; one must not publish outside one's field.

Longinus has also left a timeless reminder to those who would judge that they not lose perspective of the most important things. Our view of a magnificent forest should not be lessened by a few inferior trees. This is urgently critical in the case of those who judge music contests, for the very adjudication forms require them to comment on all the unimportant things to begin with. Longinus discusses this principle as follows:

> For my part, I am well aware that lofty genius is far removed from flawlessness; for invariable accuracy incurs the risk of pettiness, and in the sublime, as in great fortunes, there must be something which is overlooked. It may be necessarily the case that low and average natures remain as a rule free from failing and in greater safety because they never run the risk or seek to scale the heights, while great endowments prove insecure because of their very greatness.
>
> In the second place, I am not ignorant that it naturally happens that the worse side of human character is always the more easily recognized, and that the memory of errors remains indelible, while that of excellences quickly dies away.
>
> I have myself noted not a few errors on the part of Homer and other writers of the greatest distinction, and the slips they have made afford me anything but pleasure. Still I do not term them willful errors, but rather oversights of a random and casual kind, due to neglect and introduced with all the heedlessness of genius. Consequently I do not waver in my view that excellences higher in quality, even if not sustained throughout, should always on a comparison be voted the first place, because of their sheer elevation of spirit if for no other reason …
>
> It is true that Bacchylides and Ion are faultless and entirely elegant writers of the polished school, while Pindar and Sophocles, although at times they burn everything before them as it were in their swift career, are often extinguished unaccountably and fail most lamentably. But would anyone in his senses regard all the compositions of Ion put together as an equivalent for the single play of the *Oedipus*?[2]

The second-century philosopher, Sextus Empiricus, asks the question whether anyone at all is capable of judging art. First, following the line of reasoning of Anacharsis the Scythian (sixth century BC), he asks, should the expert or non-expert be the judge? Rejecting the idea of having non-experts judge as absurd, he next asks, can an expert in one art judge work in another art? No, for this judge would also be a non-expert in that art. The remaining possibility is for an expert to judge work in the same art in which he is an expert. But this too, he questions.

> Who is he that judges those who stand on the same level inasmuch as they are engaged in the same art? And besides, if this fellow-craftsman judges that one, the same thing will be both judging and judged, both trusted and distrusted; for in so far as the other man is a fellow-craftsman of the man who is being judged, he himself also will be subject to judgment and distrusted, whereas, in so far as he is giving judgment, he will be trusted. But it is not possible for the same thing to be both judging and judged, trusted and distrusted. Therefore there is none who judges by rules of art.[3]

Empiricus gives another reason why art cannot be judged, this time quoting the views of Protagoras of Abdera (490–420 BC), who asserts that everything is really just a matter of opinion,

---

[2] Longinus, *On the Sublime*, XXXII.

[3] Sextus Empiricus, 'Against the Logicians,' trans. R. G. Bury (London: Heinemann, 1935), 31.

all sense-impressions and opinions are true and that truth is a relative thing inasmuch as everything that has appeared to someone or been opined by someone is at once real in relation to him.[4]

Marcus Aurelius (121–180 AD) takes a complimentary point of view, proposing that every work of art must have its own inherent value, which is neither increased nor diminished by praise or criticism.

> Everything which is in any way beautiful is beautiful in itself, and terminates in itself, not having praise as part of itself. Neither worse then nor better is a thing made by being praised. I affirm this also of the things which are called beautiful by the vulgar; for example, material things and works of art. That which is really beautiful has no need of anything; not more than law, not more than truth, not more than benevolence or modesty. Which of these things is beautiful because it is praised, or spoiled by being blamed?[5]

Due to the Church's discouragement of art and their control of the dissemination of literature in general, one finds no further discussion of criticism until the romantic literature just before the Renaissance. Among the troubadours, there was one well-known for his vanity. For Peire d'Alvernhe (fl. 1150–1180), self-criticism meant self-praise. In one song he suggests he has many jealous detractors, but knows he is the best because of the money he makes, 'of which there's plenty.'

> Therefore, though they are all of one herd, they lie most softly
> between their teeth, and I feel assured of the best that is and
> that was, confident in my song and supreme over the deceivers;
> and I know what I'm saying, for otherwise the grain would
> not come of which there's plenty, in season.[6]

He adds that the careful listener will agree that his work is the best, even though it will always be subjected to criticism. The negative criticism, he says, one must simply ignore.

> Anyone for whom fine verse is pleasant to hear from me, I
> advise to listen to this one which I'm now about to sing; for
> once his heart is set on hearing well the notes and the words
> he'll never say that he ever heard finer things said in verse, near or far.
>
> It's certainly not to be mocked at if one hears it, rather should
> it be most pleasing, even though the opinions of the overweening,
> with their stupid, feeble, feckless sniggers, drag down that
> which is on high; we see that good makes its own way forward,
> while mockery stays galloping behind.
>
> Hence it is well to ignore it, for never does mockery or spite desist.[7]

---

[4] Ibid.
[5] Marcus Aurelius, *Meditations*, IV, 20.
[6] 'Sobre.l vieill trobar,' in Alan Press, *Anthology of Troubadour Lyric Poetry* (Austin: University of Texas Press, 1971), 93.
[7] 'Cui bon vers,' in Ibid., 97.

Criticism, he points out, robs even the finest artist of his confidence.

> Ah! Merit, how you are muted, deaf and squint, and Worthiness, how broken I see you and dragged to and fro! For whoever wants to so ill-treats you that a vile and wicked people, pulling and pushing and snapping, have confused and perverted you; and this robs you of sense and guidance.[8]

Among the Germanic contemporaries of the troubadours, the Minnesingers, we find two interesting objections to the critics based on the fact that the critics are incapable of knowing Truth, from the poet's individual perspective. Truth, sung from the heart, was an important part of their aesthetic values, as we see in a song by Vogelweide (1170–1230 AD).

> Many there are that mock my pain,
> And ever say that 'tis not truly from the heart I sing;
> These but spend their breath in vain,
> Since they can never yet have known love's joy and suffering;
> And so it is they judge me wrong:
> Whoever knows
> All that from true love flows,
> Would not misunderstand my song.[9]

Heinrich von Morungen (d. 1222) makes the same point, that the critic 'cannot know what drives me to sing.' His poem reminds us of the maxim, 'If you laugh, the world laughs with you; if you cry, you cry alone.'

> Many a one of them says, 'Aha! look at him singing!
> If he [really] suffered, he wouldn't do that.'
> A man like that cannot know what drives me to sing.
> But now, as in former days, I shall raise my voice.
> When I stood mute in sorrow, I was worth nothing to her.
> That is the anguish that oppresses me:
> Sorrow is despised where men rejoice.[10]

By the Renaissance we begin to find much more outspoken attacks against the critics. Giovanni Boccaccio (1313–1375), reared in Florence and Naples, was destined by his family for a career in finance, but like his great friend, Petrarch, he abandoned his profession for poetry. Boccaccio attempts to categorize some of the types of men who criticize poets and poetry. First, there are those 'madmen' who are simply arrogant and criticize everything in sight. Such men, Boccaccio finds, are usually uneducated in the subjects they profess to judge, thus his prescription for them:

---

[8] 'Belh m'es qu'ieu,' in Ibid., 95.

[9] In *Selected Poems of Walter von der Vogelweide*, trans. W. Alison Phillips (London: Smith, Elder, & Co., 1896), 43.

[10] 'Leitliche blicke und grozliche riuwe,' in Frederick Goldin, trans., *German and Italian Lyrics of the Middle Ages* (Garden City: Anchor Books, 1973), 45.

> If they really are impelled by this desire for glory, and seek a reputation for wisdom, let them go to school, listen to teachers, pore over their books, study late, learn something, frequent the halls of brilliant debaters; and lest they rush into teaching with undue haste, let them remember the Pythagorean caveat, that no one who came to his school to speak on philosophical subjects should open his mouth until he had listened for five years. When they shall win praise in this respect, and earn genuine title, then, if they wish to come forward, let them lecture, or dispute, or refute, or inveigh, and vigorously press their opponents. But any other course is proof rather of madness than wisdom.[11]

Another who criticized the poet at this time, Boccaccio tells us, was the lawyer. The lawyer, he reminds us, is interested only in money and cannot understand why anyone would desire a profession where they are destined to be poor. But, Boccaccio answers, the poet's reward is rather in wisdom and immortality.

> I readily grant therefore their contention, that poetry does not make money, and poets have always been poor—if they can be called poor who of their own accord have scorned wealth. But I do not concede that they were fools to follow the study of poetry, since I regard them as the wisest of men ...
>
> ......
>
> Furthermore, if the privilege of long life is not granted a man in any other way, poetry, at any rate, through fame vouchsafes to her followers the lasting benefit of survival—rightly enough called a benefit, since we all long for it. It is perfectly clear that the songs of poets, like the name of the composer, are almost immortal. As for lawyers, they may shine for a little while in their gorgeous apparel, but their names in most cases perish with the body.[12]

In a letter of 1548, following the death of Bembo, the famous Italian poet, Pietro Aretino (1492–1556) offers a standard he wishes the critic would observe. One should hear a work three times before judging it, 'the first time you hear a poem you listen to it, the second time you savor it, the third time you judge it.'[13] We cannot help but observe that this would be a very difficult standard to employ in the case of contemporary music, the great majority of which is never heard a second time.

The Italian philosopher, Giraldi Cinthio (1504–1573), in a letter sent to his publisher, indicated that he wrote his treatise, 'Discorso intorno al comporre dei romanzi,' of 1549, to refute attacks on Ariosto's *Orlando Furioso*, which he considered a great heroic poem. Thus, while his treatise is about the sixteenth-century heroic poem in general, which he calls the Romance, Giraldi is equally concerned with establishing poetry as an art. In so doing, he presents one of the most important treatises on Beauty to be found in the sixteenth century.

---

[11] *Genealogia Deorum Gentilium*, quoted in *Boccaccio on Poetry*, trans. Charles Osgood (New York: The Liberal Arts Press, 1956). XIV, ii.

[12] Ibid., XIV, ivff.

[13] Letter to Alessandro, in Thomas Chubb, *The Letters of Pietro Aretino* (New Haven: Shoe String Press [Archon Books], 1967), 271.

Giraldi has some interesting recommendations in this work dealing with self-criticism for the poet when his work is finished. He points out that it is good to have a respected person read it, to find what is 'displeasing in beauty.' He has found it is profitable to lay the work aside and come back to it at a later time.

> His original fervor and love for it when it was born—almost as if it were a new child—having cooled off, the author sees it as if it were not his own, so that he finds in it much to correct which his original fervor had not permitted him to see.[14]

But then again, he warns against too much correcting and editing.

> Certainly he should avoid excessive use of the file, so that the good is lost along with the bad; as someone said, he ought to know when to lift his hand from the desk, because, as I have often said, excess is bad in any undertaking.[15]

Desiderius Erasmus (1469–1536) was a great humanist, scholar and writer of prose of the sixteenth century. He was born near Rotterdam and left an orphan while still a teenager. The executor of his parents' estate, in order obtain everything for himself, gave Erasmus over to a monastic career.

Erasmus, who himself was a much criticized writer, took the understandable position that the entire idea of the critic, and the public in its role as critics, was unfair.

> The life of those who like myself write books is no better than that of the actors of antiquity who presented a play on the stage before the public. They had to learn their parts, to rehearse their production, to do all that was humanly possible to satisfy their audience—that motley throng, truly a beast of many heads, few of whose members have the same tastes, nor are they always consistent, and what is worse, the greater part of them are led by prejudice rather than judgment. On their thumbs the poor mountebank is wholly dependent; he must worship the lowest of the mob, and after superhuman exertions thinks himself happy if he has secured a hearing for his play. If he is hissed off the stage, he must find a tree and hang himself. Surely books have to face critics who are no less various, no less difficult to please, no less distorted by prejudice. In one way our fate is more unfair, in that we put on our show at our own expense, while the actors get their fee. And they, if the dance is a failure, merely look foolish; we, if we fail to please, are heretics.[16]

In a letter to a friend, Erasmus added,

> He who criticizes another man's writing gets, to begin with, as much of a name in one year as his author has acquired by the labors of many years. And then the critic is commonly thought cleverer than his victim. Last but not least, there are plenty of people to spur him on.[17]

---

[14] Giraldi Cinthio, *Discorso intorno al comporre dei romanzi*, in Henry Snuggs, *Giraldi Cinthio On Romances* (Lexington: University of Kentucky Press, 1968), 159.

[15] Ibid., 159.

[16] Letter to Pedro Ruiz de la Mota [1522], in *The Collected Works of Erasmus* (Toronto: University of Toronto Press, 1992), IX, 60.

[17] Letter to Thomas Lupset [1519], in Ibid., VII, 154.

Andreas Ornithoparchus was associated with several German universities, in particular Leipzig and Tubingen. His music treatise, *Musice active micrologus*, of 1517, was widely used as an educational text in sixteenth-century Germany. Ornithoparchus anticipated that his book would be attacked by critics and so he warns the reader to ignore them.

> I doubt not that there will be some who will snarl at it and backbite it, condemning it before they read it and disgracing it before the understand it. Some would rather seem, than be, musicians, not obeying authors, or precepts or reasons, but whatsoever comes into their hair-brain Cockscomb … To whom I beg you (gentle Readers) to lend no ear … Neither listen to those that hate the art, they who dissuade others from that which their dullness will not allow them to attain, for it is in vain to harp before an ass.[18]

By the Baroque Period, France had established its several academies, honorary institutions to govern the arts. It followed, naturally, that 'official rules' gave the critics new criteria to raise against poets, artists and composers. In 1637 Jean Chapelain published a treatise called, 'Les Sentimens de l'Academie françoise sur la Tragi-comedie du Cid.' This paper reflects an intellectual debate which followed the enormous success of Corneille's *Le Cid*, first produced in 1636. A number of jealous 'arbiters of taste' in Paris attacked the work for treating an unacceptable subject and for violating the rules of drama. After several counterattacks, including one by Corneille himself, the question was taken up by the Academy. As this discussion continued, Chapelain (1595–1674) included music as an illustration for his contention that it is not enough to please, but a work of art must also observe the rules 'of the experts'—an obvious reference to the Academy itself.

> Hence, they are at one, and we agree with them both, and we can all of us together say that a play is good when it produces a feeling of reasonable content. But, as in music and painting, we should not consider every concert and very picture good if it please the people but fail in the observance of the rules of their respective arts, and if the experts, who are the sole judges, did not by their approval confirm that of the multitude. Hence we must not say with the crowd that a poem is good merely because it pleases, unless the learned and the expert are also pleased. Indeed, it is impossible that there can be pleasure contrary to Reason, unless it be to a depraved taste—as, for instance, a liking for the bitter and the acid.[19]

Voltaire also cried against the 'official rules' which a playwright such as himself was expected to observe. Some of Voltaire's most interesting comments on critics, expressed in a combination of prose and poetry, are found in the satiric poem, 'The Temple of Taste.' Here, among inferior writers, we see the critic, the bearer of the 'official rules.' One poet, frustrated by the idea of an official Taste defined by rules, announces he will disprove the Academy premise—by virtue of ideas expressed as if they consisted of mathematics. In this Temple one finds,

---

[18] Ornithoparchus, *Musicae active mirologus* and Dowland, *Introduction: Containing the Art of Singing* (New York: Dover, 1973), 211.

[19] Quoted in Barrett Clark, *European Theories of the Drama* (New York: Crown Publishers, 1959), 125ff.

a crowd of writers of every rank, age and condition, who scratched at the door and begged of Criticism to permit them to enter. One brought with him a mathematical romance, another a speech made before the Academy; one has just composed a metaphysical comedy; another held in his hand a poetical miscellany long since printed, with a long approbation and a privilege; another presented a mandate written in an affected and over-refined style, and was surprised to find that all present laughed instead of asking his blessing. 'I am the reverend father,' said one: 'Make room for my lord,' said another.

> A prating sir, with voice acute,
> Cried, 'I'm the judge of each dispute,
> I argue, contradict and prate,
> What others like I'm sure to hate.'
> Then Criticism appearing, cried,
> 'Your merit is by none denied;
> But since Taste's godhead you reject,
> Do not to enter here expect.'

Bardou then cried out, 'The world's in error, and will always continue so; there's no God of Taste, and I'll prove it thus.' Then he laid down a proposition, divided and subdivided it; but nobody listened, and a greater multitude then ever crowded to the gate.[20]

Voltaire attacks the idea of 'official rules' again in his best-known work, *Candide*. In a passage which discusses the theater in France, Voltaire comments on those critics ['wits'] who pan a work, even though it is so effective that members of the audience cry.

> Candide found himself placed near a cluster of wits: this, however, did not prevent him from shedding tears at some parts of the piece which were most affecting, and best acted. 'You are greatly to blame to shed tears; that actress plays horribly, and the man that plays with her still worse, and the piece itself is still more execrable than the representation. The author does not understand a word of Arabic, and yet he has laid his scene in Arabia, and what is more, he is a fellow who does not believe in innate ideas. Tomorrow I will bring you a score of pamphlets that have been written against him.'[21]

Later one of the above critics speaks of the 'official rules' of writing drama.

> Whoever neglects any one of these rules, though he may write two or three tragedies with tolerable success, will never be reckoned in the number of good authors.[22]

Voltaire provides a portrait of a fictional critic in a scene in *Candide* where Candide is touring a great private library. First Candide is shown eighty volumes of memoirs of the Academy of Sciences, a symbol of the Scholastic tradition still alive at the University of Paris. His host

---

[20] 'The Temple of Taste,' in *The Works of Voltaire* (New York: St. Hubert Guild, 1901), XXXVI, 49ff. Voltaire had angered Jean Baptist Rousseau by observing of his poem 'Ode to Posterity,' that it was unlikely to reach its destination. Rousseau responded by attacking Voltaire's recent dramatic work, *Zaire*, which in turn prompted Voltaire to write 'The Temple of Taste.'

[21] *Candide*, in Ibid., I, 154ff.

[22] Ibid., 160.

observes that these volumes contain not a single article of real utility.[23] Next he is shown volumes comprising three thousand plays, of which scarcely thirty are 'worth anything.' Of huge volumes of sermons, the host admits no one, even himself, ever looks at them. The innocent Candide observes that this must be the happiest man, who owns all these books. His guide responds, no, he dislikes everything he possesses. In an exchange intended to describe critics, we find,

> CANDIDE. But there must certainly be a pleasure in criticizing everything, and in perceiving faults where others think they see beauties.
> MARTIN. That is, there is a pleasure in having no pleasure.[24]

It is clear that Voltaire, himself, personally suffered from frequent attacks on both his plays and his poetry. One poem suggests that Voltaire's own personal experience had left him rather bitter about critics of poetry. In his, 'The Three Manners,' a discourse on Greek drama and modern critics, Voltaire observes that the critics have no heart, and they come from Hell.

> Perish, perish the wretches who would censure all plays;
> When that vile, abject race first existed below,
> A heart Nature on them forgot to bestow.[25]

We sense his frustration again in a work of fiction, 'The World as it Goes,' where we find a 'man of letters,' whom we must regard as Voltaire, who speaks of the critics ('pedants').

> In all times, in all countries, and in all kinds of literature, the bad swarm and the good are rare. Thou hast received into thy house the very dregs of pedantry. In all professions, those who are least worthy of appearing are always sure to present themselves with the greatest impudence. The truly wise live among themselves in retirement and tranquility.[26]

In his poem, 'Envy,' Voltaire suggests that Rameau fared little better with the critics.

> Orpheus alone should dare to hiss Rameau;
> Venus to criticize is Psyche's right;
> But why should we in censure thus delight?
> No beauty she acquires who blames a face …[27]

In only one place does Voltaire speak well of a critic, one of the more famous critics of poetry of the French Baroque, Nicolas Boileau (1636–1711).

---

[23] Ibid., 182ff.
[24] Ibid., 182ff.
[25] 'The Three Manners,' in Ibid., XXXVI, 141.
[26] 'The World as it Goes,' in Ibid., III, 282.
[27] 'Envy,' in Ibid., XXXVI, 185. In another poem, 'To the King of Prussia,' Ibid., XXXVI, 198, Voltaire tells us that Frederick the Great, well-known to us also as a composer and flute player, had intended to compose an opera based on his military experiences.

> In Boileau we excuse satiric rage,
> Some beauties please in the malignant page.
> That bee had honey to assuage the grief
> Of those he stung, and give some kind relief.²⁸

From the English Baroque there is much extant comment on the criticism. Among this commentary there was one man, Anthony Cooper, Earl of Shaftesbury (1671–1713), who actually wrote in praise of the role of the critic.

> I take upon me absolutely to condemn the fashionable and prevailing custom of inveighing against critics as the common enemies, the pests and incendiaries of the commonwealth of Wit and Letters. I assert, on the contrary, that they are the props and pillars of this building; and that without the encouragement and propagation of such a race, we should remain as Gothic architects as ever.²⁹

The viewpoint of the poets and playwrights themselves was, of course, negative. Perhaps the most famous response by a poet to the critics, and *not* one intended as a comment on education in general, was penned by Alexander Pope (1688–1744).

> A little learning is a dangerous thing;
> Drink deep, or taste not the Pierian spring:
> There shallow draughts intoxicate the brain,
> And drinking largely sobers us again.³⁰

Another complaint is by George Wither (1588–1667), who dedicated to the critics a preface called, 'To the scornfully Censorious.'

> What have we here? says pride-puft-ignorance,
> More Poetry? yes fool; more, too, perchance,
> Then thou wilt like; and, more, for thee to jeer,
> Till foaming at thy mouth, thy brains appear
> Through witless Choler, when thy soul shall dread,
> What, thou with scornful disrespect, have read.³¹

In another prologue, to Farquhar's play, *The Twin-Rivals*, attributed to a 'Mr. Motteux,' the playwright particularly complains that the critics condemn a work before it is even before the public.

> With Drums and Trumpets in the Warring Age,
> A Martial Prologue should alarm the stage.
> New plays—before acted; A full audience near,

---

28 'Envy,' in Ibid., XXXVI, 186.

29 *Characteristics of Men, Manners, Opinions, Times*, 'Advice to an Author,' II, ii.

30 'An Essay on Criticism,' lines 215ff, in *The Works of Alexander Pope* (New York: Gordian Press, 1967), II, 47.

31 *Works of George Wither* (New York: Franklin, 1967), In his 'The Schollers Purgatory,' Wither makes a scathing attack on book publishers and book sellers. [See Ibid., Spenser Society, Nr. 12]

> Seem towns invested, when a siege they fear.
> Prologues are like a Forlorn Hope sent out
> Before the play, to skirmish, and to scout:
> Our dreadful foes the critics, when they spy
> They cock, they charge, they fire—then back they fly.

One playwright, frustrated by the harsh criticism he had experienced, thought it might be a better world if the work of critics were turned over to ladies. In the prologue, attributed to a 'Mr. Duke,' to Lee's play, *Lucius Junius Brutus*, we find,

> But oh! you leading Voters of the Pit,
> That infect others with your too much Wit,
> That well affected Members do seduce,
> And with your malice poison half the house,
> Know your ill managed Arbitrary sway,
> Shall be no more indured but ends this day.
> Rulers of abler conduct we will choose,
> And more indulgent to a trembling Muse;
> Women for ends of Government more fit,
> Women shall rule the Boxes and Pit.[32]

Thomas Betterton (1635–1710), a famous English actor, believed, as many did at the time, that the lack of interest in the professional theater was due primarily to the competing entertainment of Italian Opera. If only, he writes,

> our [critics] could distinguish between good and bad so far as to encourage the former, and explode the latter, they would soon have plays more worthy of the English genius, and opera would retire beyond the Alps.[33]

John Dryden (1631–1700), who has been called the greatest literary man of his age,[34] was born to a Puritan family and completed his university work at Cambridge. As a working playwright, Dryden often was critical of the critics, generally characterizing them as he did in his Prologue to *All for Love*, an adaptation of Shakespeare's *Antony and Cleopatra*.

> What flocks of critics hover here today,
> As vultures wait on armies for their prey,
> All gaping for the carcass of a play!

---

[32] Charles Gildon, *The Life of Mr. Thomas Betterton* [1710] (London: Frank Cass, 1970). On the other hand, in another place, [Ibid., 21] he presents a different view, pointing out that Harrington, in his *Oceana*, suggests that all women who have 'suffered any blemish to their reputation' should be excluded from the audience of plays, so as to deter them from further lewdness.

[33] Ibid., 173ff. Betterton was one of several theater people in seventeenth-century England who failed to appreciate Shakespeare.

[34] Bernard Grebanier, *English Literature* (Great Neck: Barron, 1959), 249.

In several prefaces to his plays, Dryden attacks critics for being only interested in finding minor mistakes in the works of playwrights. A typical complaint is found in the Prologue to *Tyrannick Love*.

> And malice in all critics reigns so high,
> That for small errors, they whole plays decry;
> So that to see this fondness, and that spite,
> You'd think that none but Madmen judge or write.[35]

In the second prologue of *Secret Love*, Dryden announces he will ignore the critics—which of course he never did.

> Our poet's sturdy, and will not submit.
> He'll be before-hand with them, and not stay
> To see each peevish Critick stab his play:
> Each puny censor, who his skill to boast,
> Is cheaply witty on the poets cost.[36]

No matter how strong the attacks by the critics, it can be said that most English writers of the Baroque had sufficient self-confidence to look down on the critics. Johathan Swift, for example, observed,

> When a true genius appears in the world, you may know him by this infallible sign; that the dunces are all in confederacy against him.[37]

Alexander Pope arrived at a similar conclusion.

> Were he sure to be commended by the best and most knowing, he is as sure of being envied by the worst and most ignorant, which are the majority.[38]

Pope, reminding his readers of the relative value to society of poet and critic, added,

> a bad author deserves better usage than a bad critic.

Finally, William Shenstone (1714–1736), having noticed that critics were often failed writers, finds a clever expression.

> A poet that fails in writing, becomes often a morose critic. The weak and insipid white wine makes at length excellent vinegar.[39]

---

35 *The Works of John Dryden*, ed. Edward Hooker (Berkeley: University of California Press, 1956), X, 114.
36 Ibid., IX, 120.
37 'Thoughts on Various Subjects,' in *The Prose Works of Jonathan Swift* (Oxford: Blackwell, 1957), I, 242.
38 Quoted in *The Works of Alexander Pope*, I, 4.
39 William Shenstone, *Men and Manners* (Boston: Houghton Mifflin, 1927), 46.

It was during the late English Baroque that newspaper criticism became influential. Eventually the London newspapers began to report in wide detail the daily activities of musicians and in the process preserved for us a valuable record of music making. As one illustration, when Haydn came to London in 1794 he brought with him new symphonies to be premiered there. At an early rehearsal, during which he was conducting from a keyboard instrument, he was embarrassed by the concertmaster, the first violin, who was, and is today, known in England by the name, 'Leader.' This moron violinist insisted that as 'leader' it was his responsibility to determine the tempi of Haydn's new symphonies, even though Haydn was present and the orchestra had never before seen the material. This was duly reported in the newspapers and became the subject of a brief public debate over the relative rights of the leader and conductor. Eventually Charles Burney came to Haydn's support by contributing the following to the press:

> There is a censure leveled at Haydn ... for marking the measure to his own new composition: but as even the old compositions had never been performed under his direction, in this country, till last winter, it was surely allowable for him to indicate to the orchestra the exact time in which he intended the several movements to be played, without offending the leader or subalterns of the excellent band which he had to conduct.

On the continent the early years of the nineteenth century saw the founding of several important newspapers devoted to music, foremost among them being the *Allgemeine musikalische Zeitung*. The role of the newspapers took on a new importance with the dawn of Romanticism in literature, for these writers wrote of music as if it were a religion and their style of writing captured the imagination of the public. Consider this reference to Haydn, the year after his death, in an 1810 issue of the above newspaper; does anyone describe Haydn this way anymore?

> His symphonies lead us into vast green woodlands, into a merry, gaily colored throng of happy mortals. Youths and maidens float past in a circling dance; laughing children, peering out from behind the trees, from behind the rose bushes, pelt one another playfully with flowers. A life of love, of bliss like that before the Fall, of eternal youth; no sorrow, no suffering, only a sweet melancholy yearning for the beloved object that floats along, far away, in the glow of the sunset.[40]

The enthusiasm and support of these writers was greatly responsible for helping change the image of the musician from court servant to artist. Following their lead, a number of great nineteenth-century composers also began to be involved in writing for various newspapers and journals. Most musicians today recall that Robert Schumann played a very important role as the principal writer for the *Neue Zeitschrift für Musik*. His articles introducing Chopin and Brahms to the musical world are still widely quoted. In his diary, of ca. 1833, Schumann also made a comment that we really like. He was thinking about the future and the need for a

---

[40] Issue of July, 1810, written by E. T. A. Hoffmann, in Oliver Strunk, *Source Readings in Music History* (New York: Norton, 1950), 776.

journal to defend the 'music of the future.' But who would be the editor of such a journal? He finally concludes that such a journal was so important that the only men he could think of 'fit to edit it,' were,

> the great blind cantor of the Thomas school and the great deaf Kapellmeister, who sleeps at Vienna.

That is to say, Bach and Beethoven!

Carl Maria von Weber also wrote for years for the *Allgemeine musikalische Zeitung* and later composers such as Liszt and Berlioz also wrote extensively. There are more than four hundred extant newspaper articles by Berlioz and they are great, exceeding the prose of any other commentator on music in France. Sadly, they are for the most part not available in modern editions.[41]

Richard Wagner became so active in his prose commentary that his prose efforts are now published in no fewer than eight volumes. Even if he never wrote a note of music, Wagner would have still been at least a footnote in nineteenth-century literature. In particular, as everyone knows, Wagner had a running battle with the rational and conservative Vienna critic, Eduard Hanslick, and Hanslick became immortalized as 'Beckmesser' in Wagner's opera, *Die Meistersinger*.[42]

But while all this Romantic activity was going on, there was also a parallel existence of the more traditional writers, of whom, of course, Hanslick is the best known today. These 'normal' critics were often career journalists with little background in music, attacking new music and new composers from their personal perspective and little more. Consequently, the great composers of the nineteenth century raged against these critics in their personal correspondence. Franz Liszt called them 'laggards,'[43] 'unequivocal arrogance of mediocrity'[44] and 'men of the "But" and "Yet," who set to themselves the task of crushing to death every living endeavor.'[45] In a letter of 1867, Liszt mentioned criticism in America, of which he had heard.

> It seems that, among you, the cavillings and blunders and stupidities of a criticism adulterated by ignorance, envy and venality exercises less influence than in the old continent.[46]

Robert Schumann coined a nice phrase in description of the traditional critic: 'Music induces nightingales to sing, dogs to yelp.'[47]

---

[41] For a little book we wrote on Berlioz, we literally spent years collecting about one hundred of these articles by way of microfilm copies from Europe.

[42] Wagner originally planned to call the character, Hans Lick.

[43] Franz Liszt, *Chopin*.

[44] Letter to Franz Brendel, March 18, 1855.

[45] Letter to Alexander Ritter, Dec. 4, 1856.

[46] Letter to William Mason, July 8, 1867.

[47] Schumann's Diary.

EARLY VIEWS ON CRITICISM 131

The great composers took some solace in the knowledge that, in the end, you can't please everyone. Chopin observed, 'the man has not been born who can please everyone.'[48] One wonders if, as a child, Chopin had read one of the traditional Till Eulenspiegel stories.

> One day Till's father announced to his son that he had decided to sell one of their mules and invited his son to accompany him into town.
>
> Off they went, with young Till riding on the mule. Soon they passed a group of farmers standing in a field who pointed at them and said, 'Look at that selfish boy: riding and making his poor old father walk!'
>
> So, feeling badly for Till, the father got on the mule and had Till walk. Soon they passed some peasants who whispered and pointed and said, 'Look at that heartless old man! Riding while he makes his poor young son walk!'
>
> Consequently, the father decided they should both ride, but soon some folks standing by the road said, 'Look at those cruel people—making a poor mule carry *two* people!'
>
> So, father and son got off and they proceeded to carry the mule. But soon folks were laughing, saying, 'Can you believe that! They own a mule, but instead of riding it they are carrying it!'
>
> The moral of which is, that no matter what you do in this life you can't please everyone!

Mendelssohn, rather than concentrating on the fact that you can't please everyone, focused on the futility of judging others.

> Nothing is more repugnant to me than casting blame on the nature or genius of any one; it only renders him irritable and bewildered, and does no good. No man can add one inch to his stature: in such a case all striving and toiling is vain, therefore it is best to be silent.[49]

It is very much a tribute to the memory of Franz Liszt that he went out of his way, throughout his life, to help young musicians. To young composers and writers who were wounded by the attacks of the critics, he often advised, 'Just keep going.' Two typical examples of his encouragement read,

> Moreover, dear friend, things didn't and don't go any better with other better fellows than ourselves. We need not make any fancies about it, but only go onward quietly, perseveringly, and consistently.[50]
>
> ……
>
> … the thinking and creative artist must not allow himself to be misled by [criticism], and must go his own gait quietly and undisturbed, as they say the hippopotamus does, in spite of all the arrows which rebound from his thick skin.[51]

Robert Schumann, again in his diary, once made an important definition about the class of music journalists.

---

[48] Letter to Tytus Wojciechowski, March 27, 1830.
[49] Letter to Ferdinand Hiller, Jan. 24, 1836.
[50] Letter to Louis Kohler, March 2, 1854.
[51] Letter to Eduard Liszt, March 26, 1857.

Critics and reviewers are not alike; the former stands nearer to the artist, the latter to the mechanic.

At the end of the nineteenth century a new generation of outstanding artist-critics appeared, most notably the Irish playwright, George Bernard Shaw. But after them, the twentieth century appears to us in retrospect to have been an era of mainly reviewers. And today, do we have critics or reviewers? Who do we have writing today whose efforts, like those of Shaw, will be read a century from now?

Bibliography

CHAPTER 1 MUSIC AND CHARACTER FORMATION

Anderson, Warren. D. *Ethos and Education in Greek Music*. Cambridge: Harvard University Press, 1966.
Anonymous. *Il Novellino*. Translated by Edward Storer. London: Routledge.
Aristotle. *Problemata*.
Aristotle. *Politica*.
Aristoxenus. *The Elements of Harmony*. Translated by Henry S. Macran. Hildesheim: Georg Olms Verlag, 1974.
Ascham, Roger. *The Whole Works of Roger Ascham*. Edited by Rev. Giles. London: John Russell Smith, 1864.
Athenaeus. *Deipnosophistae*.
Boethius. *Fundamentals of Music*. Translated by Calvin Bower. New Haven: Yale University Press.
Buszin, Walter. 'Luther on Music.' *Musical Quarterly* 32, no. 1 (January, 1946): 80–97, doi: 10.1093/mq/XXXII.1.80
Carpenter, Nan Cooke. *Music in the Medieval and Renaissance Universities*. Norman: University of Oklahoma Press, 1958.
Galilei, Vincenzo. *Fronimo* [1584]. Translated by Carol MacClintock. Neuhasen-Stuttgart: Hanssler-Verlag, 1985.
Herodotus. *The Histories*.
Mace, Thomas. *Musick's Monument* [1676]. Paris: Editions du Centre National de la Recherche Scientifique, 1966.
Manniche, Lise. *Music and Musicians in Ancient Egypt*. London: British Museum Press, 1991.
Marchetto of Padua. *Lucidarium*. Translated by Jan W. Herlinger. Chicago: University of Chicago Press, 1985.
Mattheson, Johann. *Der vollkommene Capellmeister* [1739]. Translated by Ernest Harriss. Ann Arbor: UMI Research Press, 1981.
Milton, John. *The Works of John Milton*. Edited by Frank Patterson. New York: Columbia University Press, 1931–1938.
Norman, Gertrude and Miriam Shrifte. *Letters of Composers*. New York, Knopf, 1946.
Palisca, Claude V. *Humanism in Italian Renaissance Musical Thought*. New Haven: Yale University Press, 1985.
Plato. *Laws*. Translated by B. Jowett. Oxford: Clarendon Press, 1953.
Plato. *Republic*
Plutarch. *Concerning Music*.

Polybius. *The Rise of the Roman Empire.*

Reader's Digest (November, 1973).

Strabo. *The Geography of Strabo.* Translated by Horace L. Jones. Cambridge: Harvard University Press, 1960.

Strunk, Oliver. *Source Readings in Music History.* New York: Norton, 1950.

Tyard, Pontus de. *Solitaire Second ou Discours de la Musique* (Lyons, 1552), in Frances Yates. *The French Academies of the Sixteenth Century.* London: University of London, 1947; Nendeln: Kraus Reprint, 1968.

Young, Edward. *Edward Young: The Complete Works.* Hildesheim: Olms, 1968.

Chapter 2 On Music and Manners

Aethenaeus. *Deipnosophistae.*

Agrippa, Henry Cornelius. *De occulta Philosophia.* In Donald Tyson, *Three Books of Occult Philosophy.* St. Paul: Llewellyn Publications, 1993.

Ascham, Roger. *The Schoolmaster* [1570]. Edited by Lawrence Ryan. Ithaca: Cornell University Press, 1967.

Bacon, Francis. *The Works of Francis Bacon.* Edited by James Spedding. Cambridge: Cambridge University Press, 1869.

Bryskett, Lodowick. *A Discourse of Civill Life.* Edited by Thomas Wright. Northridge: San Fernando Valley State College, 1970.

Buszin, Walter, 'Luther on Music,' *The Musical Quarterly* 32, no. 1 (January, 1946): 80–97, http://www.jstor.org/stable/739566.

Calvin, Jean. *Geneva Psalter.* Quoted in Oliver Strunk, *Source Readings in Music History.* New York: Norton, 1950.

Capella, Martianus. *Martianus Capella and the Seven Liberal Arts.* Translated by William Harris Stahl and Richard Johnson. New York: Columbia University Press, 1977.

Cassiodorus. *Variae.* Translated by Thomas Hodgkin. London: Frowde, 1886.

Clark, Barrett. *European Theories of the Drama.* New York: Crown, 1959.

Clement of Alexandria. *Miscellanies.* Translated by William Wilson. Edinburgh: T. & T. Clark, 1884.

Erasmus, Desiderius. *Opera omnia.* Edited by J. Clericus, quoted in Clement A. Miller, 'Erasmus on Music,' *The Musical Quarterly* 52, no. 3(July, 1966): 332–349, http://www.jstor.org/stable/3085961.

Hooker, Richard. *The Works of Mr. Richard Hooker.* Oxford: Clarendon Press, 1888.

Hucbald, Guido, and John on Music. Translated by Warren Babb. New Haven: Yale University Press, 1978.

Johannes de Garlandia. *De Mensurabili Musica.* Translated by Stanley Birnbaum. Colorado Springs: Colorado Collge Music Press, 1978.

Kristeller, Paul. 'Music and Learning in the Early Italian Renaissance.' *The Journal of Renaissance and Baroque Music* 1, no. 4 (1947): 255–274, http://www.jstor.org/stable/20528744.

Kuhnau, Johann. *Der musicalische Quack-Salber*. Dresden, 1700.

Listenius, Nicolaus. *Musica*. Translated by Albert Seay. Colorado Springs: Colorado College Music Press, 1975.

Lucretius. *On the Nature of the Universe.*

Mace, Thomas. *Musick's Monument* [1676]. Paris: Editions du Centre National de la Recherche Scientifique, 1966.

Medieval Lore. Translated by Robert Steele. London: Stock, 1893.

Mersenne, Marin. *Harmonie universelle* (1636).

Milton, John. *The Works of John Milton*. Edited by Frank Patterson. New York: Columbia University Press, 1931–1938.

Montaigne, Michel. *Essays*. Translated by M. A. Screech. London: Penguin, 1993.

Ornithoparchus. *Musicae active mirologus* and Dowland, *Introduction: Containing the Art of Singing*. New York: Dover, 1973.

Palisca, Claude V. *Humanism in Italian Renaissance Musical Thought*. New Haven: Yale University Press, 1985.

Pirrotta, Nino. 'Music and Cultural Tendencies in 15th-Century Italy.' *Journal of the American Musicological Society* 19, no. 2 (1966): 127–161, http://www.jstor.org/stable/830579.

Plato. *Timaeus.*

Plutarch. *Customs of the Lacedaemonians.*

Porphyry. *Life of Pythagoras*. Translated by Kenneth Guthrie, *The Pythagorean Sourcebook*. Grand Rapids: Phanes Press, 1987.

Quintilian. *The Education of an Orator (Institutio Oratoria)*. Translated by H. E. Butler. London: Heinemann, 1938.

Sextus Empiricus, 'Against the Musicians,' in *Against the Professors*. Translated by R. G. Bury. Cambridge: Harvard University Press, 1949.

Vives, Juan. *Vives: On Education*. Translated by Foster Watson. Cambridge: University Press, 1913.

Wagner, Richard. *Wagner's Prose Works*. Translated by William Ashton Ellis. New York: Broude.

Yates, Frances. *The French Academies of the Sixteenth Century*. London: University of London, 1947; Nendeln: Kraus Reprint, 1968.

Chapter 3 On the Character of the Performer

Agrippa, Henry Cornelius. In *De occulta Philosophia*, in Donald Tyson, *Three Books of Occult Philosophy*. St. Paul: Llewellyn Publications, 1993.

Buszin, Walter, 'Luther on Music,' *The Musical Quarterly* 32, no. 1 (January, 1946): 80–97, http://www.jstor.org/stable/739566.

Cervantes, Miguel. *The Trials of Persiles and Sigismunda*. Translated by Celia Weller and Clark Colahan. Berkeley: University of California Press, 1989.

de Rojas, Fernando. *La Celestina*. Translated by J. M. Cohen. New York: New York University Press, 1966.

Galilei, 'Dialogo della musica antica e della moderna,' in Oliver Strunk. *Source Readings in Music History*. New York: Norton, 1950.

Lope de Vega. *La Dorotea*. Translation by Alan Trueblood and Edwin Honig. Cambridge: Harvard University Press, 1985.

Miller, Clement. *Hieronymus Cardanus, Writings on Music*. American Institute of Musicology, 1973.

Milton, John. *The Works of John Milton*. Edited by Frank Patterson. New York: Columbia University Press, 1931–1938.

Montaigne, Michel. *Essays*. Translated by M. A. Screech. London: Penguin, 1993.

Ore, Oystein. *Cardano The Gambling Scholar*. New York: Dover, 1953.

Plato. *Laws*.

St. Basil. *Exegetic Homilies*. Translated by Sister Agnes Way. Washington, D.C.: The Catholic University of America Press.

Strabo. *The Geography of Strabo*. Translted by H. L. Jones. Cambridge: Harvard University Press, 1960.

Wright, Craig. 'Performance Practices at the Cathedral of Cambrai 1475–1550.' *The Musical Quarterly* 64, no. 3 (July 1978): 295–328, http://www.jstor.org/stable/741504.

Chapter 4 Women not Allowed!

Aretino, Pietro. *The Letters of Pietro Aretino*. New Haven: Shoe String Press [Archon Books], 1967.

Ascham, Roger. *The Whole Works of Roger Ascham*. Edited by Rev. Giles. London: John Russell Smith, 1864.

Athenaeus. *Deipnosophista*.

Boccaccio, Giovanni. *Concerning Famous Women*. Translated by Guido Guarino. New Brunswick: Rutgers University Press, 1963.

Boccaccio, Giovanni. *The Corbaccio*. Translated by Anthony Cassell. Urbana: University of Illinois Press, 1975.

Brant, Sebastian. *The Ship of Fools*. Translated by Edwin Zeydel. New York: Columbia University Press, 1944.

Bruno, Giordano. *Cause, Principle and Unity*. Translated by Jack Lindsay. New York: International Publishers, 1962.

Bryskett, Lodowick. *A Discourse of Civill Life*. Edited by Thomas Wright. Northridge: San Fernando Valley State College, 1970.

Castiglione, Baldassare. *The Courtier*. Translated by George Bull. New York: Penguin Books, 1967.

Chamberlin, Henry H. *Last Flowers*. Cambridge: Harvard University Press, 1937.

Erasmus, Desiderius. *The Collected Works of Erasmus*. Toronto: University of Toronto Press, 1992.

Farmer, Henry G., 'The Music of Ancient Egypt,' in *New Oxford History of Music*. London: Oxford University Press, 1966.

Gower, John. *The Voice of One Crying*. Translated by Eric Stockton in *The Major Latin Works of John Gower*. Seattle: University of Washington Press, 1962.

Greene, Robert. *The Life and Complete Works of Robert Greene*. Edited by Alexander Grosart. New York: Russell & Russell, 1964.

Herodotus. *The Histories*.

Homer. *Odyssey*.

Lactantius. 'The Divine Institutes.' Translated by William Fletcher in *The Works of Lactantius*. Edinburgh: T. & T. Clark, 1886.

Lope de Vega. *La Dorotea*. Translated by Alan Trueblood and Edwin Honig. Cambridge: Harvard University Press, 1985.

Machaut. *The Judgment of the King of Navarre*. Translated by James Wimsatt and William Kibler. Athens: The University of Georgia Press, 1988

Magnus, Albertus. *De Animalibus*. Translated by James Scanlan. Binghamton, NY: Medieval & Renaissance Texts, 1987.

Montaigne, Michel de. *Essays*. Translated by M. A. Screech. London: Penguin, 1993.

Morley, Henry. *Ideal Commonwealths*. Port Washington: Kennikat Press, 1968.

Plato. *Laws*.

Plato. *Republic*.

Sendrey, Alfred. *Music in the Social and Religious Life of Antiquity*. Rutherford: Fairleigh Dickinson University Press, 1974.

Sidney, Philip. *The Prose Works of Sir Philip Sidney*. Edited by Albert Feuillerat. Cambridge: Cambridge University Press, 1962.

Strunk, Oliver. *Source Readings in Music History*. New York: Norton, 1950.

Chapter 5 The Ancient Artist and the Public

Aesop. *Aesop*. Translated by Lloyd W. Daly. New York: Yoseloff, 1961.

Aristotle. *Poetics*.

Athenaeus. *Deipnosophistae*.

Barker, Andrew. *Greek Musical Writings*. Cambridge: Cambridge University Press, 1989.

Bede. *Ecclesiastical History of England*. Translated by J. A. Giles. London: Bohn, 1849.

Cassidorus. *Variae*. Translated by Thomas Hodgkin. London: Frowde, 1886.
Cicero. Brutus.
Cicero. *Brutus*.
Cicero. *Pro Archia Poeta*.
Cicero. *Pro Sestio*.
Cicero. Tusculan Disputations.
Clement of Alexandria. *The Miscellanies*. Translated by William Wilson. Edinburgh: T. & T. Clark, 1884.
Horace, *The Art of Poetry*.
Horace. *Epistles*.
Horace. *Odes*.
Julian. *The Works of the Emperor Julian*. Translated by Wilmer Wright. London: Heinemann, 1913.
Lactantius. *The Divine Institutes*. Translated by William Fletcher in *The Works of Lactantius*. Edinburgh: T. & T. Clark, 1871.
Pickard-Cambridge, Arthur. *The Dramatic Festivals of Athens*. Oxford: Clarendon Press, 1953.
Plato. *Laws*.
Plato. *Phdaerus*.
Plato. *Republic*.
Plato. *Symposium*.
Pliny the Y9unger. *The Letters of the Younger Pliny*. New York: Penguin, 1985.
Robinson, T. M. *Heraclitus*. Toronto: University of Toronto Press, 1987.
Suetonius. *The Twelve Caesars*. New York: Penguin, 1989.

Chapter 6 The Renaissance Artists and the Public

Anonymous. *Lazarillo de Tormes*. In Angel Flores, ed., *Masterpieces of he Spanish Golden Age*. New York: Holt, Reinhart, 1963.
Bruno, Giordano. *The Expulsion of the Triumphant Beast*. Translated by Arthur Imerti. New Brunswick: Rutgers University Press, 1964.
Camoes, Luis. *The Lusiads*. Translated by Richard Fanshawe [1655]. Edited by Geoffrey Bullough. Carbondale: Southern Illinois University Press, 1963.
Castiglione, Baldassare. *The Courtier*. Translated by George Bull. New York: Penguin Books, 1967.
Cervantes, Miguel. *Don Quijote*. Translated by Burton Raffel. New York: Norton, 1995.
Chubb, Thomas. *The Letters of Pietro Aretino*. New Haven: Shoe String Press [Archon Books], 1967.
Erasmus, Desiderius. *The Collected Works of Erasmus*. Toronto: University of Toronto Press, 1992.

Galilei, Vincenzo. *Fronimo* [1584]. Translated by Carol MacClintock. Neuhasen-Stuttgart: Hanssler-Verlag, 1985.
Glarean. *Dodecachordon*. Translated by Clement Miller. American Institute of Musicology, 1965.
Guicciardini, Francesco. *Maxims and Reflections*. Translated by Mario Domandi. New York: Harper Torchbooks, 1965.
Lope de Vega. *Five Plays*. New York: HIll and Wang, 1961.
Lope de Vega. *Lo fingido verdadero*. Translated by Michael McGaha. San Antonio: Trinity University Press, 1986.
Luther, Martin. *Luther's Works*. St. Louis: Concordia, 1961.
Montaigne, Michel. *Essays*. Translated by M. A. Screech. London: Penguin, 1993.
More, Thomas. *The Complete Works of St. Thomas More*. New Haven: Yale University Press, 1984.
Nashe, Thomas. *The Works of Thomas Nashe*. Edited by Ronald McKerrow. Oxford: Blackwell, 1966.
Petrarch, Francesco. *Letters from Petrarch*. Translated by Morris Bishop. Bloomington: Indiana University Press, 1966.
Petrarch, Francesco. *Petrarch's Lyric Poems*. Translated by Robert Durling. Cambridge: Harvard University Press, 1976.
Robinson, James. *Petrarch, The First Modern Scholar and Man of Letters*. New York: Putnam, 1914.
Petrarch, Francesco. *Remedies for Fortune Fair and Foul*. Translated by Conrad Rawski. Bloomington: Indiana University Press, 1991.
Tasso, Torquato. *Creation of the World*. Translated by Joseph Tusiani. Binghamton: Center for Medieval & Early Renaissance Studies, 1982.
Vida. *The Art of Poetry*. In Albert Cook, *The Poetical Treatises of Horace, Vida, and Boileau*. Boston: Ginn, 1892.
Vives, Juan. *Introduction ad Sapientiam*, in Marian Tobriner, ed., *Introduction to Wisdom*. New York: Teachers College Press, 1968.
Zarlino, Gioseffo. *On the Modes*. Translated by Vered Cohen. New Haven: Yale University Press, 1983.

CHAPTER 7 THE BAROQUE ARTISTS AND THE PUBLIC

Addison, Joseph. *Remarks on Several Parts of Italy in 1701*. London, 1705.
Bianconi, Lorenzo. *Music in the Seventeenth Century*. Translated by David Bryant. Cambridge: Cambridge University Press, 1987.
Browne, Thomas. *Sir Thomas Browne's Works*. Edited by Simon Wilkin. London: Pickering, 1836.

Burney, Charles. *Memoirs of the Life and Writings of the Abate Metastasio.* New York: Da Capo Press, 1971.

Evelyn, John. *Diary.* London, 1907.

Kendall. *Vivaldi.* London: Granada Publishing, 1979.

La Bruyere. *Characters.* Translated by Jean Stewart. Baltimore: Penguin Books, 1970.

Marivaux. *The Virtuous Orphan.* Translated by Mary Collyer. Carbondale: Southern Illinois University Press, 1965.

Mattheson, Johann. *Das Neu-Eröffnete Orchestre.* Hamburg, 1713.

Misson, F. M. *A New Voyage to Italy.* London, 1695.

Penn, William. *The Select Works of William Penn.* London: William Phillips, 1825.

Playford, John. *An Introduction to the Skill of Music* [1674]. Ridgewood: Gregg Press, 1966.

Rosand, Ellen. 'Venice, 1580–1680.' In *The Early Baroque Era.* Englewood Cliffs: Prentice Hall, 1994.

Shenstone, William. *Men and Manners.* Boston: Houghton Mifflin, 1927.

Tosi, P. F. *Observations on the Florid Song.* London: Wilcox, 1743.

Voltaire. *Select Letters of Voltaire.* Theodore Besterman. London: Nelson, 1963.

Voltaire. *The Selected Letters of Voltaire.* Translated by Richard Brooks. New York: New York University Press, 1973.

Voltaire. *The Works of Voltaire.* New York: St. Hubert Guild, 1901.

CHAPTER 8 THE NINETEENTH CENTURY ARTISTS AND THE PUBLIC

Carter, Richard, 'An Interview with Antal Dorati,' *The Instrumentalist.* December, 1980.

Finn, William J. *The Conductor Raises his Baton.* London: Dobson, 1946.

Fuchs, Peter Paul. *The Psychology of Conducting.* New York: MCA, 1969.

Liszt, Franz. *Chopin.* 1852.

Schumann, Robert. *Diary* [ca. 1833].

Shapiro, Nat. *An Encyclopedia of Quotations about Music.* New York: Da Capo Press, 1978.

Wagner, Richard. *Richard Wagner's Prose Works.* Translated by William Ellis. New York: Broude.

Walter, Bruno. *Of Music and Music-Making* (New York: Norton, 1957.

Weingartner, Felix. *On Conducting.* New York: Kalmus.

CHAPTER 9 EARLY VIEWS ON CRITICISM

Boccaccio. *Boccaccio on Poetry.* Translated by Charles Osgood. New York: The Liberal Arts Press, 1956.

Chubb, Thomas. *The Letters of Pietro Aretino.* New Haven: Shoe String Press [Archon Books].

Clark, Barrett. *European Theories of the Drama.* New York: Crown Publishers, 1959.

Cooper, Anthony, Earl of Shaftesbury. *Characteristics of Men, Manners, Opinions, Times.*

Dryden, John. *The Works of John Dryden*. Edited by Edward Hooker. Berkeley: University of California Press, 1956.
Erasmus, Desiderius. *The Collected Works of Erasmus*. Toronto: University of Toronto Press, 1992.
Gildon, Charles. *The Life of Mr. Thomas Betterton* [1710]. London: Frank Cass, 1970.
Goldin, Frederick, trans. *German and Italian Lyrics of the Middle Ages*. Garden City: Anchor Books, 1973.
Grebanier, Bernard. *English Literature*. Great Neck: Barron, 1959.
Liszt, Franz. *Chopin*.
Longinus. *On the Sublime*.
Marcus Aurelius. *Meditations*.
Ornithoparchus. *Musicae active mirologus,* and Dowland. *Introduction: Containing the Art of Singing*. New York: Dover, 1973.
Pliny. *Natural History*.
Pope, Alexander. *The Works of Alexander Pope*. New York: Gordian Press, 1967.
Press, Alan. *Anthology of Troubadour Lyric Poetry*. Austin: University of Texas Press, 1971.
Sextus Empiricus. *Against the Logicians*. Translated by R. G. Bury. London: Heinemann, 1935.
Shenstone, William. *Men and Manners*. Boston: Houghton Mifflin, 1927.
Snuggs, Henry. *Giraldi Cinthio On Romances*. Lexington: University of Kentucky Press, 1968.
Strunk, Oliver. *Source Readings in Music History*. New York: Norton, 1950.
Swift, Jonathan. *The Prose Works of Jonathan Swift*. Oxford: Blackwell, 1957.
Vogelweide, Walter von der. *Selected Poems of Walter von der Vogelweide*. Translated by W. Alison Phillips. London: Smith, Elder, & Co., 1896.
Voltaire. *The Works of Voltaire*. New York: St. Hubert Guild, 1901.
Wither, George. *Works of George Wither*. New York: Franklin, 1967.

About the Author

Dr. David Whitwell is a graduate ('with distinction') of the University of Michigan and the Catholic University of America, Washington DC (PhD, Musicology, Distinguished Alumni Award, 2000) and has studied conducting with Eugene Ormandy and at the Akademie für Musik, Vienna. Prior to coming to Northridge, Dr. Whitwell participated in concerts throughout the United States and Asia as Associate First Horn in the USAF Band and Orchestra in Washington DC, and in recitals throughout South America in cooperation with the United States State Department.

At the California State University, Northridge, which is in Los Angeles, Dr. Whitwell developed the CSUN Wind Ensemble into an ensemble of international reputation, with international tours to Europe in 1981 and 1989 and to Japan in 1984. The CSUN Wind Ensemble has made professional studio recordings for BBC (London), the Köln Westdeutscher Rundfunk (Germany), NOS National Radio (The Netherlands), Zürich Radio (Switzerland), the Television Broadcasting System (Japan) as well as for the United States State Department for broadcast on its 'Voice of America' program. The CSUN Wind Ensemble's recording with the Mirecourt Trio in 1982 was named the 'Record of the Year' by The Village Voice. Composers who have guest conducted Whitwell's ensembles include Aaron Copland, Ernest Krenek, Alan Hovhaness, Morton Gould, Karel Husa, Frank Erickson and Vaclav Nelhybel.

Dr. Whitwell has been a guest professor in 100 different universities and conservatories throughout the United States and in 23 foreign countries (most recently in China, in an elite school housed in the Forbidden City). Guest conducting experiences have included the Philadelphia Orchestra, Seattle Symphony Orchestra, the Czech Radio Orchestras of Brno and Bratislava, The National Youth Orchestra of Israel, as well as resident wind ensembles in Russia, Israel, Austria, Switzerland, Germany, England, Wales, The Netherlands, Portugal, Peru, Korea, Japan, Taiwan, Canada and the United States.

He is a past president of the College Band Directors National Association, a member of the Prasidium of the International Society for the Promotion of Band Music, and was a member of the founding board of directors of the World Association for Symphonic Bands and Ensembles (WASBE). In 1964 he was made an honorary life member of Kappa Kappa Psi, a national professional music fraternity. In September, 2001, he was a delegate to the UNESCO Conference on Global Music in Tokyo. He has been knighted by sovereign organizations in France, Portugal and Scotland and has been awarded the gold medal of Kerkrade, The Netherlands, and the silver medal of Wangen, Germany, the highest honor given wind conductors in the United States, the medal of the Academy of Wind and Percussion Arts (National Band Association) and the highest honor given wind conductors in Austria, the gold medal of the Austrian Band Association. He is a member of the Hall of Fame of the California Music Educators Association.

Dr. Whitwell's publications include more than 127 articles on wind literature including publications in Music and Letters (London), the London Musical Times, the Mozart-Jahrbuch (Salzburg), and 52 books, among which is his 13-volume *History and Literature of the Wind Band and Wind Ensemble* and an 8-volume series on *Aesthetics in Music*. In addition to numerous modern editions of early wind band music his original compositions include 5 symphonies.

David Whitwell was named as one of six men who have determined the course of American bands during the second half of the 20th century, in the definitive history, *The Twentieth Century American Wind Band* (Meredith Music).

A doctoral dissertation by German Gonzales (2007, Arizona State University) is dedicated to the life and conducting career of David Whitwell through the year 1977. David Whitwell is one of nine men described by Paula A. Crider in *The Conductor's Legacy* (Chicago: GIA, 2010) as 'the legendary conductors' of the 20th century.

> 'I can't imagine the 2nd half of the 20th century—without David Whitwell and what he has given to all of the rest of us.' Frederick Fennell (1993)

About the Editor

CRAIG DABELSTEIN began studying the piano at age seven and took up the saxophone at age twelve. Mr Dabelstein has Bachelor of Arts (Music) and Bachelor of Music degrees from the Queensland Conservatorium of Music, where he majored in the performance of classical saxophone repertoire. He also has a Graduate Diploma of Learning and Teaching and a Graduate Certificate in Editing and Publishing from the University of Southern Queensland.

He has held the principal alto and tenor saxophone chairs in the Australian Wind Orchestra and has been an augmenting member of the Queensland Philharmonic Orchestra, the Queensland Symphony Orchestra, and the Queensland Pops Orchestra. For many years he was also a member of the Queensland Saxophone Quartet.

He has been a casual conductor of the Young Conservatorium Symphonic Winds, and has previously been a saxophone teacher at the Queensland Conservatorium of Music. He is a regular conductor of the Queensland Wind Orchestra, having served as their artistic director and chief conductor from 2004 to 2009.

Craig Dabelstein is a research associate for the *Teaching Music Through Performance in Band* series of books, contributing analyses to volumes 7, 8, 1 (rev. edn), and the *Solos with Wind Band Accompaniment* volume. He served as the copyeditor and layout designer of the *Australian Clarinet and Saxophone Magazine* from 2007 to 2009 and he has written many CD and book reviews for *Music Forum* magazine. He is the editor of the second editions of the books by Dr. David Whitwell including *A Concise History of the Wind Band*, *Foundations of Music Education*, *Music Education of the Future*, *The Sousa Oral History Project*, *Wagner on Bands*, *Berlioz on Bands*, *The Art of Musical Conducting*, and the *Aesthetics of Music* series (8 volumes) and *The History and Literature of the Wind Band and Wind Ensemble* series (13 volumes). From 1994 to 2012 he was a staff member at Brisbane Girls Grammar School. He now teaches woodwinds and conducts bands at St. Joseph's College, Gregory Terrace, Brisbane, Australia.

www.ingramcontent.com/pod-product-compliance
Lightning Source LLC
Chambersburg PA
CBHW080552230426
43663CB00015B/2805